east of boston

D0855108

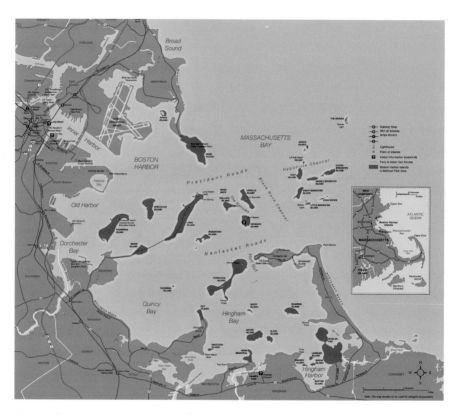

A map of the Boston Harbor Islands National Park Area. *Courtesy of the Boston Harbor Islands Alliance.*

east of boston

NOTES FROM THE HARBOR ISLANDS

Stephanie Schorow

Charleston | London

THE
History
PRESS

Published by The History Press
Charleston, SC 29403
www.historypress.net

Cover design by Marshall Hudson.
All images courtesy of the author unless otherwise noted.

First published 2008

Manufactured in the United Kingdom

ISBN 978.1.59629.379.3

Library of Congress Cataloging-in-Publication Data

Schorow, Stephanie.
East of Boston : notes from the Harbor Islands / Stephanie Schorow.
p. cm.
Includes bibliographical references.
ISBN 978-1-59629-379-3
1. Boston Harbor Islands (Mass.)--History. 2. Boston Harbor Islands (Mass.)--Guidebooks. 3. Boston Harbor Islands (Mass.)--Anecdotes. 4. Schorow, Stephanie--Travel--Massachusetts--Boston Harbor Islands. 5. Boston Harbor Islands (Mass.)--Description and travel. I. Title.
F73.63.S36 2008
974.4'6--dc22
2008015019

contents

acknowledgements

I t would be difficult to name all the people who so graciously shared their memories and their research on the Boston Harbor Islands. Many park rangers, volunteers and visitors willingly gave up time to talk to a pesky reporter; any mistakes in these pages are the fault of the writer, not her sources. I would like to thank (in no particular order) Suzanne Gall Marsh, Carol Fithian, Claire and Bill Hale, Judy McDevitt, Tom Powers, Kelly Fellner, Diane Haynes, Elizabeth Carella, Carol Thistle, Valerie Wilcox, Ellen Berkland, Tom Loring, Eleanor Cutting, Sally Snowman, Bob Enos, Walter Enos, Bruce Jacobson, Richie Sutherland, Matt Hillman, Lawrence Walsh, Allen Gontz, Robert Dillon, Brett, Richard "Baldy" Murphy, Sheila Martel, Steven Marcus, Susan Kane, Kathy Abbott, Michael Madej, Nancy Martin, Kristen Sherman and Mary Eng, for her title suggestion. Also Mary Keith and Erin Schleigh of the MFA, Victoria Stevens of the Hull Lifesaving Museum and Carole Anne Meehan of the ICA. I'm also very grateful to the library staff of the *Boston Herald* for their patience, Renee DeKona for her photography input, Paul Stevenson for his Photoshop lessons, Aaron Schmidt for his help at the Boston Public Library and Paul Christian, Michael Gerry and Ted Gerber for their information and encouragement. Many thanks to Kathy Alpert for her postcard expertise, and to Kathryn Jacob for telling me about the Great Brewster diary. An extremely huge shout-out goes to Melissa Cook for her editing skills and excellent suggestions. Thanks go to Bill and Mary Stevenson, who took me on that first boat trip, and Linda Kincaid for sending me on my first island assignment. As always, I'm eternally indebted to Alice Templeton and Marsha Turin, who were always being dragged to the islands. I especially want to thank Saunders Robinson of The History Press and Shawna Mullen, who gave me an excuse to spend my summer camping on the islands of Boston Harbor.

CHAPTER 1

welcome to the islands

The Boston Harbor Islands form a transition between the open ocean and the settled coast, between the world beyond Boston Harbor and the features specific to it.
    —Boston Harbor Islands: A National Park Area, *general management plan*

This book is a guide, a history and a love letter. It was written in the heat of fresh passion, a time when a relationship is flush with the sense of discovery. But like any letter written by an ardent wooer of a coy mistress, it's a bit peevish at times. Most passionate affairs are a mixture of infatuation, adoration, impatience and frustration. So is this one. Perhaps it seems strange that the object of my affection is a series of dots in the ocean, small islands in Boston Harbor within sight of the city, islands that since 1996 have been gathered into a most unusual national park.

Yet these thirty-four islands (actually islands, former islands and peninsulas) have been beloved by generations of New Englanders. Their history reaches back to the beginnings of Boston, when those prickly, uptight Puritans grabbed a bit of rocky coast and decided to build a city on a hill. Before these immigrants arrived, the islands were the territory of Native Americans, who fished and gathered food along their shores. Like today's island campers, they gazed over the ocean, pondering deep questions of existence: What is my purpose in life? What's over the horizon? What's for dinner?

As happens in many affairs, my relationship with the Boston Harbor Islands began through a coincidence. I'm not a Boston native (although I can say *wicked smaaht* with the best of them), but like many converts, I've become a booster of the "Hub," with its Revolutionary War history, do-gooder spirit, incomprehensible traffic patterns and madcap drivers. Like many city residents, I had only a vague idea that there were islands in Boston Harbor—that much-maligned waterway now undergoing restoration. For

The tidal pools around Lovells Island invite exploration. In the distance are Nixes Mate and the skyline of Boston.

years I saw the islands only when I took off in a plane from Logan Airport, which, as I later learned, assimilated some of the islands like a land-based alien Borg Collective—resistance being futile. Then, one day in early 2001, friends who are ardent sailors invited me along on a cruise of the harbor with their boating club.

I'm not a big fan of boats. Oh, I love the sea and relish the feeling of getting away from it all, taking a salty journey where you get to say *Aargh* a lot. Truth be told, however, I'd rather be hiking on my own two feet with a pack on my back. Not to mention there's something about being a neophyte on a boat that brings out the Captain Ahab in everyone else. *Tie that. Hold out. Not that way. This way.* Whatever. But my friends bribed me with a fine picnic lunch, so I was happy to bundle up and watch the shore rush by. The boat departed from Hingham and wove its way around Boston Harbor. We passed Spectacle Island, then undergoing its metamorphosis into habitability. It used to be a garbage dump, I was told, so packed with junk that it would spontaneously catch fire. Now the two humps of the island were as bare as a baby's bottom. "This is where the dirt from the Big Dig is going," my friends explained.

The boat rounded Georges Island, its Civil War–era fort in view. "Ever hear the ghost story about the Lady in Black?" my friends asked. The sun was starting to set as we passed a long, narrow island and a curious red brick structure sitting totally exposed on its beach. This was Lovells Island, my friends explained. The island looked wild, mysterious, deserted, its rocky shores bordered by thick trees and foliage. That strange little shack was the only visible evidence of past habitation. "You can camp on that island," my friends said.

Camp on an island! As a hiker and backpacker, I was intrigued. But how would I get back out here? "Oh, you can catch boats out to the islands," my friends informed me. "There's a main ferry to Georges Island and water shuttles among Lovells, Grape, Peddocks and Bumpkin. It's all part of the Boston Harbor Islands National Park."

Yes, now I remembered. I had read about the creation of one of the most unusual national parks in the nation, an "island park." Before we hit shore that night, I was planning a camping trip. Then as a reporter for the *Boston Herald*, I knew what I must do: convince my editors to send me there on assignment.

First I did my homework. Not only are there a number of excellent books on the islands, but the Internet also has great sources of information. There are the "official" websites of the National Park Service, the Boston Harbor Islands Alliance and the City of Boston, as well as information provided by the Volunteers and Friends of the Boston Harbor Islands, a nonprofit organization that has been working on behalf of the islands for thirty years. As I gathered information, another world opened up.

The area that we call Boston Harbor stretches from Deer Island in the northeast, through Dorchester Bay and Quincy Bay, to Point Allerton on the Nantasket Beach peninsula, which sticks out like a crooked arm into Hingham Bay. The Boston Harbor National Park Area encompasses much of an ancient field of drumlins, or hills, left in the shape of inverted spoons by the movement of glaciers. The islands are a part of the only drumlin "swarm" in the United States that intersects a coastline, a rare phenomenon that makes geologists all hot and bothered. A scant ten thousand years ago, you could walk all the way out to Little Brewster Island without getting even your toes wet. Then, as glaciers receded from North America, the sea rose and the tops of the drumlins became islands, their smooth, humped contours a contrast to the jagged, rocky islands formed from Cambridge Argillite, also found off the shores of Boston. Even before we messy humans started mucking around, the islands were undergoing constant change, with nature shaping, shifting and sculpting the shorelines and redirecting the flow of channels and currents.

Highway to the Past: The Archeology of the Big Dig, a brochure published by the Massachusetts Historical Commission, describes what the first human inhabitants of this area might have seen:

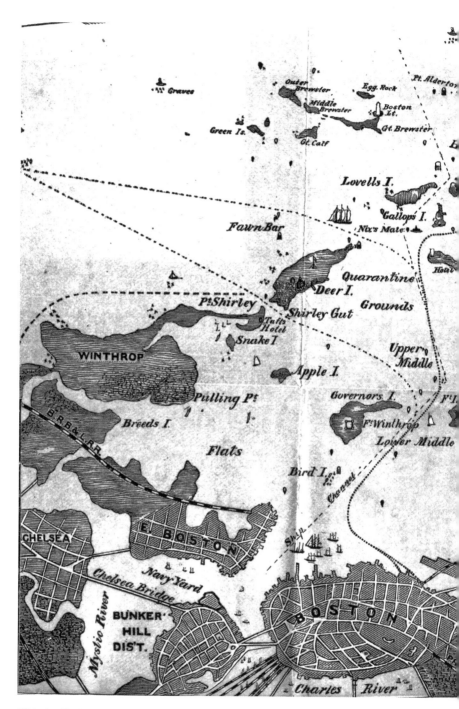

This detail of an 1882 map of the Boston Harbor, published in the "Stranger's Guide to Boston" by the Photo/Electrotype Co., Boston, shows the era's common sea routes. Because so much of Boston Harbor has been filled in, the map may look unfamiliar to modern eyes.

Imagine yourself a Native visitor to the Boston area 8,000 to 10,000 years ago. You would have come here by dugout canoe or on foot. Standing on top of what is now Spectacle Island, if you looked to the east, you would have seen a broad coastal plain, extending about 11 miles to the ocean's edge. Dotting this forested plane would be hilltops that we now know as the Boston Harbor Islands and the three major river valleys formed by what are now known as the Charles, Mystic, and Neponset rivers. As a hunter you would see the advantage of the hilltops as lookouts for spying game. As a gatherer of wild plant foods, you would see the hilltops for their blueberries, hickory nuts, and acorns. As a fisherman, you would look to the rivers, ponds, and oceans.

As the hilltops became islands, the native people continued to travel there in the warmer months. For thousands of years, they dug in the shores for clams, gathered berries, built weirs for trapping fish, hunted deer and other animals and pulled out clay for pottery. It took only a couple hundred years for Europeans to denude the islands of trees, decimate the animal population, introduce invasive species and poison the earth on at least two of the islands. This is called "civilization."

When the Europeans began to arrive in great numbers in the early 1600s, the islands were repurposed. They were shorn of their native maple, hemlock, oak, pine and hickory trees, and the logs were shipped to the mainland. Farmers then planted fields of grain and vegetables or grazed cattle. Due to their strategic location in a time of sea power, the islands became sites for forts and military outposts, their towers used to keep watch for enemies of the Commonwealth. Over the years, the islands held hospitals, almshouses, prisons, hotels and garbage dumps. They were home to the super rich, poor fishermen, eccentrics and hermits seeking only seagulls and sky for company. As James H. Stark, in his 1879 *Illustrated History of Boston Harbor*, rhapsodized: "Places that a short time since showed no more signs of human habitation than the coast of Labrador, and seemingly as forsaken as when the white man first put his foot upon these shores, are now dotted with villas and hotels, and frequented during the summer months by thousands of visitors." As Boston and surrounding communities pushed their borders into the Atlantic with landfill, some islands became part of the mainland and the shape of the harbor itself changed dramatically.

Today the Harbor Islands may seem remote, distant and way "out there" to residents of Boston and its suburbs. And indeed, many of the islands once were used for institutions deemed to be more appropriate away from the city's population. We forget, however, that in the days when masted schooners and steamships were a major form of transportation, the islands were roadside stops, tucked into the cloverleafs of watery freeways on the way to Europe and other stops along the coastal United States. Indeed, "Nantasket Roads" is the name of the channel between Georges and Hull; "President Roads" cuts between Deer and Long Island. Look at the 1882 map on pages 12 and 13, and you'll see the old ship routes and islands that, compared with the modern map in the front of this book, look far different today.

But as Boston turned from its seafaring past, the islands were largely forgotten by city dwellers. By the late 1950s, most of the islands were deserted. Once-fine homes, forts, hospitals and other buildings were destroyed, burned or crumbling. People now took planes to Europe, not boats, and nuclear weaponry had made the concept of an island fort decidedly quaint. Most of the social institutions, save those on Long Island and Deer Island, were abandoned. Slowly the islands started returning to the state they were in before the colonists came. Shrub oak started taking over the ramparts, staghorn sumac grew between the cracks in decaying roadways and poison ivy claimed the interiors of stone buildings. Spectacle Island, used as a garbage dump, was closed to additional dumping, but toxins continued to leak into increasingly polluted waters. On Peddocks

A visit to the Boston Harbor Islands is a family adventure for this father and daughter.

Island, the descendants of Portuguese fishermen clung tenaciously to the houses their grandparents built, sometimes just coming back for long summers. Locals continued to visit the islands, to fish, explore, picnic and camp, but increasingly newcomers saw Boston Harbor as merely something to view from a condo on the waterfront. The evocative names stayed on the map—Spectacle, Grape, Bumpkin, Hangman Island, Hypocrite Channel—even as the harbor itself grew filthy from the expanding city.

The islands had always been the property of various public and private entities. With the twentieth-century demand for seafront real estate, they might have been snapped up by private developers and closed to the general public. But starting in the 1970s, various groups and individuals realized that the islands—with their natural beauty and unusual history—were a resource that should be held by the people, for the people. The Commonwealth of Massachusetts started to acquire the islands in the late 1960s, establishing the Boston Harbor Islands State Park in the early 1970s. But why not, advocates began to wonder, gather *all* the islands into a national park for future generations to enjoy? One barrier, however, was the mishmash of owners and operators. State agencies controlled Grape, Bumpkin and Lovells. The City of Boston owned Long and Moon; Thompson Island was owned by an educational institution. The Trustees of the Reservation looked after the historic Worlds End park, while Little Brewster was the territory of the U.S. Coast Guard, which maintained the historic Boston Light lighthouse. And few of these agencies wanted to sell to the federal government, even for the sake of a national park.

Then in the 1990s, the idea of a national park that would not actually be owned by the National Park Service was born. Various entities would continue to keep "their" island or islands, but the National Park Service would administer the overall park and, many hoped, bring an influx of money and expertise—especially money.

In November 1996, an act of Congress created the Boston Harbor Island National Park Area, which would encompass thirty-four islands and land parks ranging in size from 1 to 240 acres, with a total of 1,600 acres at high tide, 3,500 at low tide and about thirty-five miles of shore land. An "islands partnership" was created to administer this park. Now pay attention, because this is where it gets complicated. There are thirteen members of the Boston Harbor Islands Partnership. They are representatives from the Department of Conservation and Recreation, or DCR (two seats); the Massachusetts Water Resources Authority, or MWRA; the Massachusetts Port Authority; the Trustees of Reservation; the Thompson Island Outward Bound Education Center; the Boston Office of Environmental & Energy Services; the Boston Redevelopment Authority; the United States Coast

The distinctive tower of Boston Light marks the oldest lighthouse station in the United States.

Guard; the National Park Service; the Island Alliance; and the Boston Harbor Islands Advisory Council (two seats).

And it gets even more complicated. The twenty-eight-member Boston Harbor Islands Advisory Council represents various segments of the community chosen to help guide decisions about the park's future. And the Island Alliance—renamed the Boston Harbor Islands Alliance in 2008— was formed to help raise money and awareness of the islands as well as "market" the national park.

Got all that? As an official put it to me once, "You see a lot of different uniforms out there on the islands."

Does the system work? Yes. And no. Well, most of the time, yes. Thomas Powers, president of the Boston Harbor Islands Alliance, is fond of saying, "It works better than you might think." Having said that, he also acknowledges, "Partnerships can be hard." Like most nonprofit agencies, there's always a scramble for money. This being Massachusetts, bureaucratic turf battles tend to rear their ugly heads. In 2003, then–Massachusetts Governor Mitt Romney moved to dismantle the longtime Metropolitan District Commission that oversaw Massachusetts parks, decrying it as a haven for plush patronage jobs. The parks operations of the MDC and the Department of Environmental Management were then merged—more or less—and a new Department of Conservation and Recreation was created.

Further adding to the picture are the various advocacy groups. Chief among them is the Volunteers and Friends of the Boston Harbor Islands, founded in 1979, whose members include former park rangers, longtime park visitors and others who have spent years going to the islands. Also speaking up on Boston Harbor issues is the Boston Harbor Association, founded in 1973, which focuses on promoting Boston's shoreline and harbor, and Save the Harbor/Save the Bay, a political action organization that has pushed for the cleanup of the waters of Boston Harbor. Like any good watchdog group should do, these entities often nip at the heels of the park's administration, something annoying but often necessary to keep the wheels of democracy turning.

The park has more constituents still, among them naturalists, wildlife biologists, bird-watchers and unrepentant tree-huggers like myself who see the islands as the home of plant, animal, bird and marine life whose "rights" should be considered along with those of the human visitors. There are also historians, journalists, archaeologists and other social scientists who have delved into the islands' history, seeking to preserve what has been almost lost. Native Americans want the country never to forget the terrible wrongs done to their ancestors here in the name of

Historian, radio personality and raconteur Edward Rowe Snow often took groups on tours of the Boston Harbor Islands. His enthusiasm and energy were driving forces in their preservation. *Courtesy of* Boston Herald.

civilization and Christianity. And then there are the tourists, who just want to have a nice day at the beach.

I had yet to learn all this when I planned my first trip. Back then, all I wanted was a place to camp. At that point, I had to call two different agencies for camping permits; the process has now been streamlined through the Reserve America system. Back then, I found I could camp overnight on four of the islands: Lovells, Grape, Bumpkin and Peddocks. (Peddocks is currently closed for camping.) Only Georges (and later Spectacle) had running water for public use. I got my permits and made my plans.

Within a few weeks of my first glimpse of Lovells, I was loading my pack and grabbing a taxi from the *Boston Herald* to a ferry that would take me to Georges for my first solo island-hopping trip. I spent three nights and four days visiting islands in the harbor. I found that each island was unique. Each had a different tale to tell—each provoked a different feeling or experience. You just have to listen. On that first trip, Lovells, Georges, Grape, Bumpkin and Peddocks each started talking to me, and they haven't stopped yet.

I have since visited others. Even though the islands, particularly Georges and Spectacle, can be packed on busy weekends, I found that I, a simple landlubber who thinks of port as a wine that goes with chocolate, could feel like I was on my own private island. Over the years, I returned whenever I could. The more I visited the islands, the more I wanted to visit them. The more I learned about their history—and this is a process that will go on for years—the more I wanted to know.

But the more I visited, the more concerned I became for the fate of the park. I encountered numerous glitches, complaints and concerns. I watched as the promised reopening of Spectacle was delayed over and over again; and I was frustrated to see Peddocks closed to camping and its spectacular fort closed to the public out of safety concerns. Every time I talked to someone about Gallops Island, he or she told me what a great place it was, and yet Gallops remains closed for the foreseeable future. For a few tense months, it even appeared that one of the islands, Outer Brewster, would be turned into a liquefied natural gas storage tank; some of my fellow newspaper pundits dismissed the place as just an outhouse for gulls. Volunteers, with far more experience than me, privately expressed misgivings about official decisions, while park administrators acknowledged that their plans and dreams for the islands had to face the harsh realities of limited funding. In the fall, I had a long talk with a former island shuttle operator whose ties to the islands go back to the 1960s, when he worked on boats with his father; he observed that the number of islands open to the general public seems to be decreasing, not increasing.

More people needed to know about the islands, I concluded. And not just about the islands themselves, but also about the challenges they face. So in the summer of 2007 I returned for another period of island hopping, supplemented with interviews and additional research. The result is this book.

Perhaps you may be as I was in 2001, a New Englander with only a vague knowledge of the Harbor Islands and their history. Or perhaps you're a newcomer or a visitor to Boston, bewildered by its snarling highways, lack

A view of Peddocks Island and some of the buildings of Fort Andrews.

of street signs and strange pronunciations. You'd like to experience Boston fully and perhaps visit its harbor, but you don't know how to do it or what to expect. Or maybe you have been visiting the islands for years, but you are always eager to know a little bit more.

This book is meant to be a brief introduction to the islands in Boston Harbor. Their history—both natural and human—is too long for any one volume, but these pages may give you a bit of what the islands have to offer. I won't be taking an encyclopedic approach—many of the little islands within the borders of the park will only get a passing reference. There are many excellent histories of particular islands or of a particular aspect of harbor history, from shipwrecks to lighthouses and plant life to military forts; you'll find references to them within the text and they are listed in the sources on page 155.

These pages will focus instead on the islands that are currently served by public water ferries and those frequently visited via group tours. This is an island-hopping adventure for landlubbers, those of us without boats. Don't expect to find a discussion on all thirty-four islands in the Boston Harbor National Park; many of them are accessible only by private boat or kayak. These pages will concentrate on islands that a single parent with kids, a feisty grandmother or your visiting cousins from Des Moines can visit with ease.

You might think, after reading this book or any of the other accounts of Boston Harbor history, that every inch of the islands has been pored over by historians, archaeologists and naturalists. That's not the case. Every time I venture out to their shores, I feel a keen sense of discovery, of being an intrepid explorer, of seeing something for the first time.

The Boston Harbor Islands National Park Area is at a crucial juncture. In an economic and political climate of decreased public revenues and increased pressure for development, the park must find a way to keep pace with public demands. The Island Partnership has developed a comprehensive, far-reaching "General Management Plan," but adequate funding remains elusive. Always, there is the concern that visitation must be managed; no one wants these islands to be loved to death, to be overridden by hordes of careless tourists.

The islands need our help. We have used and abused them for hundreds of years. It's give-back time.

For some reason, everyone who falls in love with the Boston Harbor Islands has one island in particular that speaks to him or her. You hear a whisper: This is your island, your place. I pestered many of those I interviewed with the same question: Which is your favorite island? Some readily discussed their favorites, and they ranged widely. One volunteer simply said, "Whenever I'm asked that, I say, 'The island I'm on right now.'" So you might ask, which is my favorite? Is it my first love, Lovells? Is it Grape, one of the most exquisite? Is it Peddocks, with its history, shifting landscape and controversies? Is it an island that I could not legally set foot on, Gallops?

Let's do some island hopping and see. We start with the basics.

CHAPTER 2

where's the buried treasure? and other frequently asked questions

Q: How many islands are there in the Boston Harbor Islands National Park Area?
A: This is kind of a trick question, as some of the "islands" in the park are peninsulas, and some of those were former islands. Let's just say there are thirty-four entities in the park.

Here's the list: Georges, Peddocks, Bumpkin, Grape, Lovells, Spectacle, Little Brewster, Outer Brewster, Middle Brewster, Great Brewster, Little Calf, Calf, Green, Slate, Raccoon, Rainsford, Gallops, Moon, Long, Thompson, Shag Rocks, Snake, Langlee, Sarah, Ragged, Sheep, Hangman, Button, the Graves, Nut, Deer, Nixes Mate, Worlds End and Webb Memorial State Park.

Q: How do I get out to the Boston Harbor Islands?
A: From May to November, high-speed ferries run to Georges and Spectacle Islands from a dock at Long Wharf near Christopher Columbus Park in downtown Boston (close to the New England Aquarium). During the late spring and summer, the boats usually run from 9:00 a.m. to 5:00 p.m. daily. During the fall, the boats operate on weekends and holidays. From Georges, you can catch the inter-island shuttle to Grape, Bumpkin, Peddocks and Lovells, with connections to Pemberton Point in Hull and the Hingham Shipyard. Ferries may also be available from the Quincy Shipyard to Georges Island in 2008. And yes, the boat schedule can seem confusing, but there are often volunteers on the islands or on Long Wharf ready to help you out.

Be aware that the schedule and routes change yearly, so always double-check the schedule posted at the general website of the Boston Harbor Islands National Park Area (www.bostonislands.com) or call 617.223.8666.

The Boston Harbor Islands may seem like a tropical paradise in the summer—even though they are just minutes away from downtown Boston.

The website also has directions to the various shipyards and information about parking. The boats run rain or shine, although trips may be canceled in very stormy weather.

The private company Harbor Express currently provides the public transportation to the Boston Harbor Islands; contact the company at 617.222.6999 or www.harborexpress.com. Harbor Express has daily sunset cruises of the harbor and whale watches and also runs MBTA commuter boats between Quincy and Long Wharf, Boston, and elsewhere.

Boston Harbor Cruises also offers harbor jaunts, ranging from whale watching to lighthouse excursions to sunset cruises; the company also operates MBTA commuter boats between Hingham and Rowes Wharf, Boston, and elsewhere. Contact the company at 617.227.4321 or www.bostonharborcruises.com.

The Hingham Shipyard is accessible off Lincoln Street (3A) in Hingham, or via the MBTA and Hingham Bus 220 to Hewitts Cove. For maps and other information, go to www.mbta.com/schedules_and_maps/boats/.

The Quincy Shipyard can be reached via Route 3A in Quincy. Directions are posted at http://www.harborexpress.com/commuters/Directions.shtml.

Q: What about the other islands?
A: Thompson is privately owned and open to the public only on Sundays during the spring and summer; boats run from the EDIC pier near Black Falcon Terminal. Rangers often offer tours of Thompson leaving from Spectacle. Check www.bostonislands.com or www.thompsonisland.org for current schedules, ticket prices and directions.

The National Park Service leads tours to Little Brewster and Boston Light from June to October. The boats leave from Fan Pier, near the corner of Atlantic Avenue and Northern Avenue in downtown Boston. Check www.bostonislands.com for schedules and current prices. You can also find information at the National Park Service site (www.nps.gov/boha) or by writing to Boston Harbor Islands Partnership, 408 Atlantic Avenue, Suite 228, Boston, MA 02110. The island's floating dock is scheduled for work in 2008, so check ahead of time to see if tours are running.

If you are interested in Rainsford, Calf, Great Brewster and other islands not served by ferry service, check for special tours posted on www.bostonislands.com. Groups that often organize excursions to these islands include the Volunteers and Friends of the Boston Harbor, 349 Lincoln Street, Hingham, MA 02043; 781.740.4290; fax 781.749.9924; e-mail fbhi@earthlink.net; www.fbhi.org.

Moon and Long Islands are off limits to the general public.

As for the others, they can, for the most part, be reached by motorboats, sailboats, kayaks and other small craft. Kayaking is a popular way to visit the islands and there are places around Boston to rent kayaks or join kayaking tours.

Boston looms up behind the rise of Spectacle and Peddocks Islands, showing how close the Harbor Islands are to the hustle and bustle of the city.

Q: How about driving?
A: You can drive to Nut Island, Worlds End, Deer Island and Webb Memorial State Park. Deer Island can be reached through the town of Winthrop; Worlds End, Nut and Webb Memorial State Park are accessible via Route 3A.

Q. How much will a visit to the islands cost?
A: Round-trip tickets for ferry service to Georges and Spectacle are (as of 2008): adults $14; children under three, free; children three to eleven $8; seniors and students $10. In 2008, a $3 ticket will be required for the inter-island shuttle service. Thus, for example, an advance round-trip ticket to Lovells Island, leaving from Long Wharf and catching the shuttle at Georges, is $17 for an adult. Group rates are also available. If you leave from Hingham, you pay the round-trip fare without the extra charge for the inter-island shuttle service. In 2008, for the first time, Harbor Express plans to offer ticket sales online.

There are no admission charges on the islands except for a $5 general admission charge to Worlds End.

Q: I've been waiting fifteen minutes. Where's the darn boat?
A: First, take a chill pill. Pretend for a minute you're *not* in Boston traffic. Boats, being subject to all kinds of problems—from weather to passengers who suddenly realize they forgot to get off at the right stop—are often delayed. Try to be patient and go with the flow. Best thing to do is plan

for extra time and contingencies. Having said that, there continues to be concern about transportation issues. If you do encounter problems, write a thoughtful, detailed letter to park officials about what happened and your suggestions for better service. E-mail boha_information@nps.gov.

Q: How do I get to Long Wharf?
A: Long Wharf is easily accessible via the MBTA. The closest subway stop is Aquarium on the Blue Line, which is easily reached via the other subway lines. Parking is available at Fan Pier or at other parking garages. Some parking garages may validate parking for National Park Service tours, so check ahead.

Q: How long does it take to get out to the islands?
A: The boat ride from Long Wharf to Spectacle takes about ten to fifteen minutes; the ride to Georges takes twenty to thirty minutes.

Q: I just want to go on a boat ride. Can I do that?
A: Sure. Many people just want to ride the ferry to and from Georges or ride the inter-island shuttle around the harbor. You can stay on the boat and never touch land until you're done for the day if you want to, just as long as you buy the ticket.

Q: I have my own boat. What will it cost me to tie up for the day or night?
A: Spectacle Island has about sixty-seven slips for boats. As of 2008, the daily docking fee for boats less than thirty feet is $20. For boats more than thirty feet, the fee is $30. The overnight fee for boats is $1.75 per foot. Overnight boaters on Spectacle may use the facilities at the Visitor Center but are limited to the dock after the park closes for the day. Slips at Georges Island are available on a first-come, first-served basis. Grape, Bumpkin, Lovells and Peddocks allow drop-offs only at their docks; visitors must anchor offshore and use dinghies to get to these islands.

Q: Are there public bathrooms on the islands?
A: There are toilets on Spectacle and Georges and outhouses on the other islands. Spectacle also has beach showers. The land parks also have facilities.

Q: Where can I swim?
A: Spectacle has a sandy beach with lifeguards on duty during the summer months. Lovells has a popular rocky beach on its eastern shore but there is no lifeguard supervision there at the current time. The currents in the harbor can be dangerous, so it is advisable to take caution even when wading.

Although the days of sail are long gone, Boston Harbor has a lot of boat traffic, from pleasure craft to fishing vessels to huge tankers to commuter boats.

Q: Can I get drinking water on the islands?

A: There are drinking fountains on Georges and Spectacle, and bottled water is for sale at snack bars and on the boats. Otherwise, please be sure to bring your own.

Q: Can I buy food on the islands?

A: Food is available for sale only on Georges and Spectacle Islands, and on the boats.

Q: Which islands can I camp on? How do I make reservations?

A: Currently, you may camp overnight on Lovells, Grape and Bumpkin. To reserve a camping site, contact Reserve America at 877.422.6762 or www. reserveamerica.com. There are between ten and fifteen individual sites and one to two group sites on each of the islands where camping is permitted. Remember, there are no showers, fresh water, electricity or telephones and certainly no food or camping supply stores. Plan accordingly. The park recommends that campers bring one gallon of drinking water per person for each day on the island.

Park officials encourage campers to catch the boats to the islands in Quincy or Hingham as overnight parking is far less expensive in the parking lots there than in Boston.

Q: Can I build a campfire?

A: Campfires are only permitted on the shore below the high-tide mark.

Q: I'm a hot dog and hamburger kind of guy. Can I bring a grill to the islands?

A: Yes, but only if they are of quality and easy to carry. However, the park has a carry on/carry off policy: all items brought onto the islands must also be taken off; this includes any charcoal briquettes, whether new or used.

Q: Can I bring my dog?

A: No. No pets are allowed on the islands. Kids are perfectly all right, however. And you can walk your dog on a leash at Deer Island, Nut Island and Webb Memorial State Park.

Q: What's up with the apostrophe in the names of the islands? Some maps use it (as in Peddock's Island, George's Island, Lovell's Island) but this book doesn't. Do you have something against the apostrophe?

A. The spelling of the names of the Boston Harbor Islands has varied over the years. Gallops was originally called Gallup's, Bumpkin has been called Bompkin and Peddocks has even been designated Petticks. However, the National Park Service made a decision to formalize the island names, without apostrophes, to indicate that they are place names. This book follows the park service style, but using an apostrophe in "Lovell's," "George's" and "Peddock's" is also correct.

Q: Where's the buried treasure?

A: If I knew, I wouldn't tell you.

Q: Which island has the fort on it?

A: Actually, several islands have the remains of military forts; but you probably mean Georges Island, which has the famous Civil War–era Fort Warren. Peddocks and Lovells, as well as other islands, also have remains of military fortifications.

Q: How many people visit the park each year? Does it get crowded?

A. Overall, the park gets about 300,000 "visits" each season. As for crowds, yes, on weekends and holidays, Georges and Spectacle can be packed. The other islands tend to get fewer visitors in general. If you can, try to visit during the week.

Q: Can I bring beer and wine to the islands?
A. Oh, you had to ask. No. No alcohol is permitted or sold on the islands, although you can buy alcoholic drinks on the boats that serve the islands. However, if you are a responsible adult over twenty-one and happen to enjoy a form of fortified grape juice, and if you behave yourself properly, no one is going to question you. Indeed, one former park official, describing her vision for the park, mentioned keeping the boats running longer in the day so that people could run over to Spectacle after work with a bottle of wine and enjoy the sunset. So don't ask, don't tell is my motto. But, officially, no booze. And please act responsibly.

Q: Okay, so I'm on the islands. What do I do with the kids?
A: You mean besides walk the beach, hike the trails with self-guided tour brochures, take a tour from a ranger or volunteer, look for shells and sea glass, explore old ruins, peer into tidal pools and eat a picnic lunch? The islands also have a variety of events during the summer months, including kite flying, classical orchestra concerts, jazz concerts, storytelling, Junior Ranger programs, sailing regattas, Civil War reenactments, holiday parties, artist encampments and Native American crafts making. All family activities are free. Check www.bostonislands.com for the latest event information.

Q: But what are the islands really like?
A: For that you will have to read the rest of this book.

CHAPTER 3

ghosts, guns and garrisons on georges island

It seems as if each individual island created its own unique and mystical atmosphere through both history and natural beauty.
   –Alan Mikal, Exploring Boston Harbor in Photographs and Text, *1973*

As the ghostly figure slowly walks along a path on Georges Island, we follow him. His pale skin is the color of parchment; his tattered mariner's outfit is ivory. His feet are bare. He moves with the deliberate speed of a cat on the prowl, his eyes unfocused, taking note neither of the gaggle of adults and children walking behind him, nor of the curious stares from people passing by. I follow the ghost, this man in white, with questions in my mind. What is he feeling? What is he thinking? Don't his feet hurt? And this is art?

The "ghost" is actually performance artist Ernesto Pujol doing a piece called "The Water Cycle" for Boston's cutting edge Institute of Contemporary Art. Playing the part of a silent "water carrier," Pujol stops by a doorway in Fort Warren, the sprawling, Civil War-era fortification on the island. He reaches a pale hand to brush the fort wall; the touch leaves a rusty mark, like a bruise on his fingertips. Little kids, fascinated with this strange adult, follow in a Pied Piper fashion, their small hands now also brushing the rough-hewn walls built to protect the country against enemies from across the sea. Pujol will say later that he felt as if the fort was crying out in pain, that it seemed so solid, yet had a fragility about it. Perhaps he was hearing from the souls of the Confederate prisoners who were once housed there. Perhaps he was getting a vibration from the many ghosts reportedly seen around the fort, including a notorious Lady in Black. Or maybe he was hearing from the soul of the storyteller who made sure future generations would know all about the islands of Boston Harbor and their ghosts.

The white-clad "ghost" in this photo of Fort Warren on Georges Island is actually a performance artist who dressed as an ancient mariner and made a pilgrimage to Georges and other Boston Harbor Islands in the summer of 2007.

Certainly the man who helped save Fort Warren, Edward Rowe Snow (1902–1982), would have enjoyed the sight of an ancient mariner stalking the walls of Fort Warren, for he loved anything that brought people to Georges Island. A devoted historian of the Boston Harbor Islands and a man who knew the value of both personal research and a mighty fine ghost story, Snow worked tirelessly to preserve Fort Warren and make sure kids would be enthralled, intrigued and maybe even spooked by a visit here. For many visitors, Georges Island is the first stop on an island-hopping adventure.

Georges Island is located about seven miles from the Boston shore, between Lovells and Rainsford Islands. Much of its forty upland acres reveals the long military history of the Harbor Islands and their use as watch posts against enemies from across the sea. Yet one of the striking aspects of island history is how rigorously the Boston Harbor Islands were developed as military fortifications and how so few of them actually underwent a real battle.

When you go to Georges by the ferry from Long Wharf or by private boat, you debark at the large pier on the western side. The brick building immediately before you was once used to store mines; it now serves as a headquarters for rangers and contains bathrooms and a snack bar. Plans call for renovations to turn it into a modern visitors' center with additional facilities in the near future. Outside there are tables and a large clearing for picnicking. A booth to the left of the headquarters is usually staffed with

Edward Rowe Snow in one of the "dungeons" of Fort Warren on Georges Island, circa 1950. *Courtesy of* Boston Herald.

volunteers from the Friends of the Boston Harbor Islands, who can direct visitors and answer questions. Guided tours are available, or you can pick up a brochure for a self-guided tour.

You can walk the circumference of the fort by following paths along the shore, or you can head inside the walls through a "sallyport," an entrance once served by a drawbridge. From parade grounds inside you can wander through a labyrinth of officers' quarters, a bakery, hospital and other rooms, some in complete darkness, which makes them an irresistible challenge for Indiana Jones wannabes. The parade grounds also contain the powder magazine, where the gunpowder used in the cannons was stored. Large "wells" set into the ground once contained twelve-inch guns that would disappear when they recoiled.

One of the more popular islands, Georges is often awash with kids; it seems designed for active, imaginative youngsters, with ramparts to climb and dark hallways to explore. Parents will be pleased to see the signage that provides history lessons. Other visitors will enjoy the views, particularly the sight of Boston Light, the venerable lighthouse, from the fort's upper ramparts. With the best-preserved historical buildings of the Harbor Islands national park, Georges has been a draw for those interested in the terrible war that once tore this nation apart and pitted brother against brother. "Fort

Visitors to Georges Island will get a history lesson in military fortification.

Warren, located on this island since 1833, has more memories of the Civil War days than any other place in New England," as Snow wrote.

Originally known as Pemberton's Island (after its owner, James Pemberton), Georges's strategic importance was recognized as early as 1690, when British troops mustered there. It was named Georges Island after a seventeenth-century Boston merchant, John George, who lived on the island in the 1680s. During the Revolutionary War, it was used as an outpost first by French and then by American forces. During the War of 1812, British and American ships waged a fierce naval battle off its shores. In June of 1813, the USS *Chesapeake* and the British frigate HMS *Shannon* engaged in a punishing ship-on-ship fight that ended with the capture of the American vessel. During the combat, the mortally wounded American captain uttered his final command: "Don't give up the ship." Unfortunately, a good slogan does not a victory make.

After that war, the American government saw the need to enhance protection along its coasts, and plans were made to build a major fort on Georges. It was named Fort Warren, named for Revolutionary War hero Joseph Warren, who died in the Battle for Bunker Hill. (The name was transferred from a fortification on Governors Island.) Signs posted around the fort today detail its history and the remarkable engineering that went into its construction. Its defense system was based on seventeenth-century French fortification theories, which employed moats, earthen cover over stone and both rifle and cannon fire to produce an impregnable wall. The structure—nearly a mile long at its perimeter—was magnificent by the day's standards. Its five sides enclosed an interior parade grounds and other facilities. Granite blocks, cut and faced by hand, were floated to the island and used for the walls, which were ten feet thick in parts. The work began in 1834 and continued until 1850.

Over those decades, however, its ramparts were used mostly by Bostonians on harbor excursions. Indeed, Snow reports that when Governor John Albion Andrew visited the island in April 1861, a welcoming salute had to be delayed until soldiers could find enough ammunition. With the beginning of the Civil War, the Second Infantry, or "Tiger," Battalion arrived at Georges and got down to business, mounting cannons on the ramparts in case Southerners or their allies decided to invade Boston by sea. Soldiers of the Twelfth Massachusetts Regiment stationed at Fort Warren, singing as they worked, created the famous song "John Brown's Body" to poke fun at a fellow soldier named John Brown, who shared his name with the abolitionist who led a failed armed insurrection in 1859 at Harpers Ferry. The song's catchy tune, based on the hymn "Say, Brothers Will You Meet Us?" in turn inspired Julia Ward Howe to write "The Battle Hymn of the Republic."

A Civil War reenactment in Fort Warren on Georges Island in July of 1990. *Photo by Rose Marston, courtesy of* Boston Herald.

Soldiers make preparations for firing the guns of Fort Warren on Georges Islands. *Courtesy of* Boston Herald.

No cannons were ever fired in actual combat from Georges during the Civil War. But Confederate prisoners of war—an estimated six hundred of them—were brought to Georges to be held behind its thick walls. They included Confederate Vice-president Alexander Stephens; George Proctor Kane, a police marshal and future mayor of Baltimore; General Simon Bolivar Buckner, who had surrendered to General Grant; Lawrence Sangston, a former member of the Maryland Legislature; and James Mason and John Slidell, Confederate emissaries to Great Britain. Several Confederate prisoners were able to keep journals of their time in prison, including Alexander Stephens. He described in a later memoir of being led into his cell: "I surveyed the room. A coal fire was burning; a table and chair were in the centre; a narrow, iron, bunk-like bedstead with mattress and covering was in a corner. The floor was stone—large square blocks. I had the full realization of being a prisoner. I was alone." Compared with other prisoner of war camps, incarceration at Fort Warren was relatively benign. Prisoners were adequately fed and had access to a prison library and other amenities.

The last Civil War prisoners were released in January 1866. The fort continued to operate into the twentieth century. During the Spanish-American War, rumors persisted that the Spanish fleet would sail into Boston Harbor, putting Fort Warren on high alert. Snow reports that an observer at dusk did happen to see four ships in a single fleet and announced that Boston was under attack by the Spanish. "It turned out to be an innocent tug with three barges in tow," Snow writes. During World War I, soldiers were quartered at Fort Warren before their deployment overseas. The area of "Bastion A" was turned into a recreation hall and cinema. During World War II, soldiers kept watch on mines placed in Boston Harbor as a precaution against possible attacks by German U-boats.

As tools of warfare shifted, an island fort soon became obsolete. Fort Warren was permanently decommissioned in 1947. Another kind of battle ensued. When the General Service Administration announced plans to auction off the island, its location was eyed with great interest by a group who wanted to uses the fort's stone quarters for the storage of radioactive material. In response, the Society for the Preservation of Fort Warren was formed, with Edward Rowe Snow as its president.

By this time Snow was a Boston legend. A descendant of sea captains, he worked as a teacher and coach and had been a reconnaissance photographer during World War II. His 1935 book, *The Islands of Boston Harbor*, was followed by nearly a hundred other books and pamphlets on such topics as pirates, shipwrecks, storms and lighthouses. In the 1950s, Snow had his own radio show named "Six Bells" and he wrote a column for the *Quincy Patriot Ledger* and other newspapers. He also carried on the tradition of a "Flying Santa." For forty years he flew small planes and helicopters to lighthouses throughout New England, dropping off holiday packages for the isolated keepers and their families.

Snow recognized the importance not only of keeping Georges Island from going nuclear but also preserving its history. At a time when Boston was about to be cut up wholesale for urban development, losing its seedy but beloved Scollay Square and West End neighborhood, Snow and others believed that parts of Boston history were worth saving. Eventually the GSA agreed to turn over Georges to the Metropolitan District Commission, the forerunner of today's DCR. After restoration efforts, Fort Warren was opened to the public in the summer of 1961.

For years, Snow led group tours of the fort; contemporaries remember his deep voice and white mane of hair as he wowed children with tales of the Civil War and, more tellingly, of the Lady in Black, a legend that, he insisted, was whispered about for years at Fort Warren. (Although, he noted, he couldn't guarantee that any part of it was true.) Here's how it goes:

A young boy doesn't quite know what to make of a ghostly performance artist near Fort Warren on Georges Island.

Among the Civil War prisoners incarcerated in Fort Warren was a young lieutenant who had been married only a short time. He managed to get a message to his young wife and, being in love and extremely resourceful, she made her way to Boston, where she obtained a pistol and men's clothing. Dressed as a man, she rowed to Georges Island and, through a prearranged signal, was hoisted into the cell where her husband was held. As the pair dug an escape tunnel, the noise alerted the fort's soldiers and the scheme was exposed. The woman attempted to fire on the colonel in charge of the fort, but the gun exploded, killing her husband. The colonel had no choice but to sentence her to death as a spy. She made one last request: to be hanged in women's clothing. Her request was granted, and she went to her death dressed as a woman. Since then, however, a ghost resembling a woman wearing a long black dress has been seen around the fort. Soldiers have even been reprimanded severely for firing at a ghostly figure. You might even see her today!

At this point, by Snow's own prearranged signal, someone would jump out from behind a door and scare the bejesus out of his audience. Kids loved it.

But is the story of the Lady in Black based on a true event? Jay Schmidt, in his comprehensive 2003 book *Fort Warren: New England's Most Historic Civil War Site*, states that soldiers would taunt one another with warnings about "the Black Widow," but he otherwise debunks any possibility that a woman was hanged as a spy at Fort Warren, clad in black or not. But in "call-your-bluff-and-raise-you-one" fashion, Schmidt offers additional ghost stories from the fort based on personal interviews. Like the one about the dog that wouldn't go inside a certain bastion. Or the time in 1981 when Civil War reenactors saw a lantern passing on the parapets with no one holding it. Even if the Lady in Black isn't strictly a "true" ghost story, it has become part of the lore of the Boston Harbor Islands. So keep an eye out.

The summer season sees a host of activities on Georges, from kite flying contests to storytelling to concerts to sporting events and a sailing regatta in September. In the past, reenactors in blue and gray have staged battles from the Civil War. Today you might catch an "art" project going on, such as the visit by the ghostly "water carrier" in the summer of 2007.

Among the island's memorial markers is one dedicated to Edward Rowe Snow. And who knows? Maybe Snow's ghost makes the rounds arm in arm with the Lady in Black, hoping to spook any kid who lags behind a tour group.

CHAPTER 4

spectacle island: from trash to triumph

You might think the 114-acre Spectacle Island was named for the view from atop its two drumlins, which rise like a pair of gargantuan humpback whales from the waters of Boston Harbor. Not so, but if you walk up the winding paths to the crest of the north drumlin, you do get a spectacle. From up here, you can look back to the mainland for a view of downtown Boston. If you shift your gaze to the northeast, you can see Logan Airport and the bulbous digesters of the sewage plant on Deer Island. Turn east and you see Boston Light, the lighthouse shining day and night on Little Brewster Island. Looking southwest, you'll see Long Island, Thompson Island and, beyond them, the shores of Quincy and Hingham. And on a clear day you can see all the way to the Blue Hills on the mainland. You are 155 feet above sea level, at the highest point in the Boston Harbor Islands.

Just a few decades ago, had you been standing in this spot (if you could stand in midair, as the island at that time rose only ninety-five feet above sea level), you'd have had a sweeping view of garbage, debris and abandoned buildings. Unseen toxins would have been leeching into the ocean, and you might have smelled smoke from fires that often broke out among the heaps of refuse. A little more than a century ago, you would have been looking at barges transporting dead horses to Spectacle, which had a rendering factory that produced hides, horsehair, oil and other equine-derived products. And before then, you'd have been looking down at a quarantine hospital, resort hotels and the homes of a few hearty souls who lived and worked on Spectacle.

Today, you look down over fields of reintroduced native and nonnative flowers, shrubs and trees, a sandy beach, a marina that juts out into a sparkling harbor and a modern visitors' center graced with a long front

The visitors' center at Spectacle Island has information on the island's transformation from a dump to a gateway for island tourists, plus a snack bar and other services.

porch and—in a burst of planning genius—rocking chairs perfect for peaceful contemplation of the horizon.

Few islands demonstrate both the potential and the frustration of the Boston Harbor Islands National Park as much Spectacle, an island now reborn through a mix of modern technology and determined grit. Its rebirth was aided by one of the largest road construction projects in United States history, the Central Artery/Third Tunnel project, known locally as the Big Dig. Visitors to the island are standing (more or less) on land that was dug up from below Boston and its harbor when the elevated stretch of Interstate 93 was moved underground and a third tunnel was dug to connect the city with Logan Airport. Much of the earth displaced by the dig was transported to the island and used to "cap" Spectacle, a process that aimed to encase toxins that had festered on the island for decades. Boston Harbor may have its lost islands (see chapter nine), but Spectacle is an example of a rescued island.

The island's name is a clue to its history and to the ever-shifting topography of the harbor. The island was used by Native Americans for fishing and hunting; on the island's south end, a shell midden was found in the 1990s, which held masses of clamshells, arrowheads, pottery shards, bone beads and other artifacts. When European immigrants started arriving in the Boston area in the late 1600s, the island consisted of two drumlins connected by a narrow spit of land that was often covered by the tides.

Its shape reminded the Puritans of a pair of spectacles, hence the name. The colonists set about harvesting trees on the island and using the land for farming. In 1717, a quarantine facility was set up on the island; ships coming into the harbor were required to discharge their passengers, who were then checked for infections such as smallpox before being admitted on land. The quarantine hospital was moved to Rainsford Island in 1737.

By the early 1800s, hotels were established on the island, including "a summer resort of great popularity," as an 1898 *Boston Globe* article put it. Some hotels, however, housed less than upstanding enterprises, such as gambling and prostitution. As Edward Rowe Snow lightly wrote in his history of the Boston Harbor Islands, "A thriving business was enjoyed but the existence of certain activities and games not allowed by the city of Boston brought police raiders in the year 1857." Spectacle's hotels eventually closed down. Range lights were built on Spectacle in 1897 and more were added in the early 1900s, which, in conjunction with range lights on Lovells Island, helped with ship navigation, according to Jeremy D'Entremont in *The Lighthouses of Massachusetts*.

Spectacle's bucolic nature would not last into the twentieth century. In 1857, the N. Ward Company established a horse rendering factory on the island. The company was first formed in 1828 by Nahum (or Nathan) Ward to "recycle" the chief form of transportation in the days before the automobile, i.e., the horse. The *Boston Globe* reported in a September 14, 1890 story about the Ward factory:

It is a curious fact that before the establishment of this firm, it was the custom when horses or cattle died…to throw them into the harbor…with the idea that they would float out with the tide. The action did not seem to work very well, for although the carcasses would float down the harbor all right; when the tide turned, they would float back again. This floating backwards and forward would continue for weeks until the decomposing carcass would strand upon some island or become entangled among the pile of a wharf or the stanchions of a bridge where, as the reader can imagine, they became anything but pleasant objects for the eye to rest upon.

To interject a modern note, may I just say, "Eeeuuw."

The N. Ward Company took care of these unpleasant objects by transporting horse carcasses—about two thousand a year—in a horse "hearse" to a wharf and then to Spectacle Island, where the remains were processed into oil, leather and meat products for dogs. For years, the island was dubbed "Ward's Island," and the small settlement made up of factory workers and their families was called "Wardville." From 1882 until the

A look at Spectacle Island in 1989 before its makeover. An ancient engine on a rusting hulk of a barge is among the trash on the island. *Photo by Ted Gartland, courtesy of* Boston Herald.

early 1900s, eleven to twenty-five students, aged five to fifteen, were given their lessons in a one-room, red-painted schoolhouse on the island. Indeed, people who grew up on the island had pleasant memories of their time there. Their homes were located at a distance from the horse plant (and the later garbage dump), and residents remembered exploring, picking blackberries, swimming and gardening on what seemed like a faraway island in sight of Boston.

By 1900, the City of Boston was seeking additional locations for the garbage produced by its growing population. The longtime custom of dumping garbage in the ocean was not working—duh—and the city needed to find new dumping grounds. In October of 1901, the city council voted to establish a garbage facility in a cow pasture on Spectacle. A contract for a garbage facility eventually went out to bid in 1912.

Over the next fifty years, Spectacle became a repository for the refuse of Boston; much of the dumping occurred on the narrow spit of land between the two drumlins, and the "spectacle" shape of the island eventually disappeared with the addition of thirty-seven acres of landfill. A plant was built on the island to compress and heat the garbage and to extract valuable grease, with the remains used as more landfill. The grease extraction plant was later abandoned—although its smokestack stood on the island for decades—but a garbage facility, run under contract by various private entities, continued to operate on Spectacle. The island was often a target for complaints about "gas attacks" and nauseating stenches. "Disgusting odors are again arising from the Coleman Bros. Inc garbage incinerating plant at Spectacle Island," the *Boston Globe* declared in July of 1923. Even Boston's legendary and colorful Mayor James Michael Curley complained about the smell as well as the politics of the city's contract with Coleman Bros. "Not only is this the smelliest plant in creation when it does smell but the Coleman contract is peppered full of the tastiest little jokers. There is no redress but to go on with it as best we can," Curley told a *Boston Globe* reporter in an article dated July 21, 1922.

So the island grew bigger—and smellier. Dumping on the island was ended in 1959, after a bulldozer sunk into an oozing heap of junk and the city started taking its garbage to an incinerator plant in South Boston. For years afterward, the island remained a no man's land. Like Boston Harbor itself, once considered one of the country's most polluted waterways, Spectacle became a joke of an island, a place that was perpetually burning from spontaneous ignitions occurring within its piles of trash. Former Boston Fire Commissioner Paul Christian remembers "looking over at nighttime and seeing the entire profile of the island outlined in flames." Fires were difficult to fight there because of the dangerous terrain from the unstable ground and rats were "as big as cats," he said in an e-mail exchange with me. "There was always a haze of smoke over dumps but no one ever minded as long as it wasn't too bad," former Boston Fire Commissioner Leo D. Stapleton recalled in his 1982 memoir, *Thirty Years on the Line.* "Occasionally though, the fire would break out of the pile and spread, creating foul-smelling clouds of dense black smoke. In the case of Spectacle Island, or 'Speckie' as it's called, once a fire broke out, the smoke would travel toward Long Island (and its hospital) in one direction." Stapleton described one memorable Fourth of July in 1955 when a fire on Speckie rained debris on picnickers at South Boston's Castle Island Park. Firefighters sent to Spectacle saw "heavy smoke pierced by long tongues of flame, leaping skyward." The men had to wade through swarms of rats and insects to get water on the fire, and two jakes nearly panicked when they started to sink into the burning rubbish. Before the fire was brought

The shoreline of Spectacle Island, which is often dotted with pottery shards and sea glass, provides evidence of its past history as a city garbage dump.

under control, much of the island was burned, including its range lights, according to Stapleton.

Visitors to the island in the 1960s and 1970s remember the huge amounts of broken glass, colored marbles, doorknobs and other debris on its shore. In his 1973 book *Exploring Boston Harbor*, Alan Mikal wrote, "A musical sound, similar to that made by chimes dangling in the wind, can be heard all along the beach. It is caused by waves from passing motorboats that wash the beach-glass gently back and forth upon the rocks, creating a high-pitched symphonic echo."

For decades Spectacle sat and stank, slowly reclaimed by vegetation and large numbers of muskrats and other rodents. Heavy metals and other toxins, meanwhile, leeched into Boston Harbor, contributing their share to the harbor's pollution.

A confluence of events helped rescue Spectacle. Planners realized the Big Dig was going to create landfill, and lots of it. Why not use it to reclaim Spectacle Island? Beginning in the 1980s, the Commonwealth and various agencies began the long process of sealing and capping Spectacle, in effect creating a whole new island.

This being Boston, any good idea is subjected to a hundred controversies. Indeed, the renovation project was delayed by numerous problems. The engineering challenges were huge, compounded by an offshore worksite. An estimated 3.7 million cubic yards of fill from the Big Dig were ferried to the islands. Workers had to dig 65 feet below sea level to build a 1,650-foot-long dike to prevent heavy metals from leeching out. Sea walls, totaling about 3,000 feet, were built in sections around the islands. Fierce discussions ensued over what to plant in the new earth: native species or a mixture of native and nonnative plants and shrubs that would quickly take root.

Opening dates were announced, only to be withdrawn. There was bickering over which agency was responsible for which tasks. Even in 2005, when Spectacle was about to really truly open, leaks in the island's cap were found; park officials refused to take the keys to the new visitors' center from the agencies doing the reclaiming work, fearing they would be held liable for a job that had not been finished. For island advocates, many of whom volunteered time and effort in the cleanup, the delays were agonizing. Finally, in 2006, Spectacle was opened for visitors. And to the amazement of many, even the most dubious, the island was a wonderful sight. That Spectacle opened to the public at all is astounding. That it is as beautiful as it is seems miraculous.

Visitors debarking at the long pier are greeted by the sight of a sandy beach, a marina with slips for boats and a modern $5 million visitors' center. The center has multimedia exhibits, a snack bar, composting toilets and running water. Five miles of trails now run over and around the island's two drumlins. The park also uses "green" energy for its facilities and vehicles. Its sandy beach, with outside showers and lifeguards, now attracts hundreds of visitors eager to swim in the once-dreaded Boston Harbor. The island's broad, paved paths can accommodate groups of eager children as well as individuals with physical challenges. Picnic tables, gazebos and benches are strategically located around the island.

A self-guided trail directs visitors to the remains of four granite blocks, the remnants of the dock for Ward's horse rendering plant. A bounty of diagrams and video interviews in the visitors' center explain the long history of Spectacle and its transformation from "Trash Island." A striking mosaic of sea glass and other objects found on Spectacle fills one wall. The island has had music concerts, educational programs and crafts workshops presented by Native Americans. Spectacle's past as a dump seems to have been totally erased. Except for one thing.

Spectacle's shore is, more than that of the other islands, littered with pottery shards, curious bric-a-brac and bits of glass now smoothed to a pale frosty glow by the tide. You will see soft green, pearly gray, deep indigo,

During peak season, Spectacle Island hosts a variety of activities, including music by local performers on the front porch of the visitor center.

pale tangerine and, if you're lucky, crimson red among the stones and shells on the sand. With the action of time and water, these discards have been softened into objects of beauty, perhaps a metaphor for Spectacle's own transformation.

From Long Wharf, it is only a ten- to fifteen-minute boat ride to Spectacle. Leave yourself at least two hours to study the exhibits in the visitors' center and walk to the top of one or both drumlins. Treat yourself to a break in one of the rocking chairs. Please note: Spectacle is a carry-on, carry-off island, so take your garbage off with you. Spectacle has had quite enough.

CHAPTER 5

lovells island: so close, and yet so far

On the Island there were…"batteries" which were cement casements covered with earth to hide the guns. These were World War I vintage guns. Two of the casements were disappearing guns…They went up in the air, fired and the firing kicked them back down. As soon as they came down, the breach was opened and another shell was put in along with a big bag of firing powder. A new cap was put on the door, the door slammed and up it went in the air again. The gun sighter would look over the top of the casement with a periscope, sight the gun and set the range. The gun captain would pull the cord and the gun would go up in the air and come back down again just as quickly as it went up. During those times we were warned not to go near the guns.

—from Harold B. Jennings, A Lighthouse Family

From atop what's left of Fort Standish on Lovells Island, I can see nature taking back what once was hers. Clambering over crumbling fortifications built in the early 1900s, I push through blackberry bushes, scrub oak and staghorn sumac, feeling as though I'm on a thousand-year-old Mayan temple in the Yucatan, not an abandoned military facility within sight of downtown Boston. Indeed, the Maya may have built better than we do today; the batteries of the fort are in various stages of ruin, their walls spider-webbed with erosion, railings bent or torn away.

But the Maya didn't have to contend with New England weather, a climate that has left its mark on the buildings, landscape, beaches and natural formations of this sixty-two-acre island between the channels of Nantasket Roads and President Roads. With its rocky beach, salt marsh and history of romance and tragedy, Lovells beckons to both overnight and day visitors. To me it is one of the more untamed of the islands; it's a wild, mysterious girl, barefoot, with briars in her hair.

A weathered staircase on one of the batteries on Lovells Island.

A trip to Lovells shows just how close the Boston Harbor Islands are, and yet how far away they make you feel. From my home in Medford, I can strap on a pack, walk out my front door and take a bus to the subway to Long Wharf. Here I can catch a ferry to Georges or Spectacle, and then take the inter-island shuttle to Lovells. Within two hours, I can be off the boat and walking down the dock to a gazebo where I check in with the rangers, pay my camping fee and chat a bit about the island.

Georges may have its Lady in Black, but Lovells has its tales of doomed lovers, shipwrecks and buried treasure. The southeastern tip is dominated by a large, open, grassy area, surrounded by old batteries, now a group camping area. Its midsection contains the remains of more batteries built into a hillside, and just beyond these is a salt marsh. The north section is heavily reforested, and the remains of military foundations here are laced with tentacles of green. The island is crisscrossed by dirt paths, boardwalks and the remains of roads, the cracking asphalt resisting erosion. On the east side of the camping area is the swimming beach, which, due to the dangerous currents in the area, is a safer place to swim. In the past this beach was supervised by lifeguards, but as of this writing, the only supervised beaches are on Spectacle. A former fire control station stands, now little more than a concrete pillar, near the beach.

My first task upon visiting Lovells for an overnight stay is to select a camping site along the western edge of the island. There are pleasant grassy sites tucked amid the trees and a few sites on the shore, just off the water's edge. On my first visit of the summer in 2007, I find my site and grapple with my tent, anchoring it with so much rope that it looks like a bug caught in a crazed spider's web. I decide it will withstand whatever wind comes off the water.

I call a *hello* to another camper, a man I'll call M, who gives the impression that he has permanently moved in. He has set up a huge tent and a sail-sized tarp supported by two oars, protection against the rain that sweeps the island. There is a solar panel charging up in the sunlight near an inflatable raft. M probably tips the scale at three hundred pounds and he sports a black eye from losing a battle with a bungee cord. A Boston Harbor Islands hat keeps his long and unruly hair flattened and apple cheeks sit above his bird's nest beard. His campsite is a jumble of gear, coolers, boxes and bags of food and some electronic devices, including a computer he runs off solar energy. M has been staying on the island for weeks (not exactly in keeping with the rules). It's soon clear that M represents a long line of colorful characters associated with the Harbor Islands.

The islands seem to attract those who choose to stray off the beaten path. One such person was the legendary Mrs. Ann Winsor Sherwin, a woman who *really* refused to give up the ship. In the 1930s, Mrs. Sherwin, a self-described poetess, and her son made their home on a four-masted freight schooner, the *Snetind*, moored off Castle Island on a coal delivery wharf. She had planned to sail the schooner around the world, but the plans for world travel never materialized. The wharf owners tried to evict Mrs. Sherwin, but she resisted, until finally the *Snetind* was cut adrift. For a time, the boat was held in place by a frozen harbor, but it eventually tore loose and stranded on Spectacle Island. The Sherwins continued to live on the wrecked hull of the ship until the 1940s; the boat eventually burned in 1947, and its shell was scuttled in the harbor.

Like a latter-day Mrs. Sherwin, M would remain on Lovells until he was asked to leave by rangers (there is a two-week limit on camping). Still, he was friendly to me and had a wealth of information about the islands. We set off together to explore.

Lovells Island was named after Captain William Lovell, an early settler of Dorchester. Lovells was farmed until it became a subpost of Fort Warren, the Civil War–era fort on Georges. In 1900, Fort Standish, named for

Fort Standish on Lovells Island shows its age.

Myles Standish, was established as part of the Endicott coastline defense system. William Crowinshield Endicott, U.S. secretary of war from 1885 to 1889, supervised changes in the American military. Under his leadership, the Endicott Board of Fortifications promoted a new approach to coastline fortification. Instead of concentrating weaponry and equipment in one heavily fortified structure (such as Fort Warren on Georges), defensive systems were to be dispersed in a series of encampments. The Spanish-American War also intensified efforts to increase the coastal defense system. Endicott fortifications were built on a number of Boston Harbor Islands, including Peddocks and Lovells, and weaponry on others, such as Georges, was beefed up.

Seven batteries were built along the eastern side of Lovells, the fortifications blending into the terrain. Battery Williams and Battery Whipple were built on the south end, surrounding a parade grounds now used as a group camping site. Battery Burbeck-Morris was cut into the central drumlin of the island to provide a place for ten-inch rifles to poke over the earthen parapet, fire and disappear upon recoil. There was a time when a crew of thirty-seven men would man guns here that could shoot nine miles into the ocean. What they would hit—besides terrified seagulls—is unknown, since the guns were never used in actual combat. After World War II, Fort Standish was decommissioned. In 1958 the MDC acquired the island and it became part of the national park in 1996.

Soldiers test the guns on one of the forts in the Harbor Islands. *Courtesy of* Boston Herald.

Because the fortifications are so overgrown, a visit to Fort Standish on Lovells is quite different from a trip to Fort Warren on Georges. For starters, there are usually fewer people here. The island's western shore is pockmarked with tidal pools and has a sweeping view of the Boston skyline. From this side, there's an excellent view of Nixes Mate (also called Nix's Mate and Nick's Mate), another landmark in Boston Harbor Islands lore.

The story goes like this: The mate of a certain Captain Nix was accused of killing his captain. Protesting his innocence, he was executed on a small island off the shores of Gallops and Lovells. The proof of his innocence, he declared, would be that the island would be washed away. And indeed, most of the land has disappeared, although erosion, not the force of justice, might be at work. The remaining rocky outcropping of Nixes Mate now holds a pyramid beacon perched on a granite base erected in 1805 by the Boston Marine Society. Once painted black, the wooden pyramid, standing about twenty feet high, is now decorated in distinctive black and white; its image is used in the logo of the Volunteers and Friends of the Boston Harbor Islands as a symbol of the group's effort to prevent the history and heritage of the islands from vanishing like the land of Nixes Mate. The tiny island has been designated a National Historic Site and the U.S. Coast Guard, which owns the beacon, restored it in 2004.

Like the Lady in Black, the tale of Nix has its doubters. In an 1880s guidebook, *King's Handbook of Boston Harbor*, author M.F. Sweetser points out that the landmass was called Nix's Island back in 1636 when its twelve acres—even then washing away—were granted to John Gallop, owner of nearby Gallops Island. This was, he wrote, long before anyone was hanged for piracy in the area. Sweetser offers an (equally implausible) alternative theory. It seems that Nix was a pirate who in 1680 sailed into Boston on a ship loaded with ill-gotten treasure. On a dark night, he and his mate went ashore on the little island and buried bags of coin. To keep the location a secret, Nix murdered his companion and buried him there as well. Sweetser offers no explanation as to how the whole story leaked out. (Perhaps a loudmouthed gull squawked?) Lawrence C. Dyer, in a *Boston Globe* article dated August 18, 1889, repeats this story and asserts it is possible that "the treasure remains buried there and some day, if not dug up, will be washed out in sight." Theories floated by other writers suggest that Gallops was once owned by a man named Nix, and that Nix's Mate referred to the small island off its shore, or that the name came from a Dutch passenger who heard the strange noises of the waves and called it "*Nixie Scmalt*," or "the wail of the water spirits" in Old Dutch.

Whatever the truth about Nix or his mate, there are eighteenth-century accounts of the other pirates, including one named William Fly, being executed and their bodies being hanged on Nixes Mate to serve as a deterrent to would-be pirates. Bird Island (now under Logan Airport) and Hangman Island in Quincy Bay were used for this purpose as well. Today Nixes Mate continues to mark the site of a treasured legend, if not actual treasure.

Certainly Lovells's crumbling structures and overgrown terrain give the impression that some kind of treasure could be buried there. While exploring the woods behind the camping area, I came across odd blocks of stone set seemingly haphazardly among the trees, as if marking some

Three views of Nixes Mate over the centuries. *Top:* A drawing of Nixes Mate representing what it looked like in 1700. From the *King's Handbook of Boston Harbor* by M.F. Sweetser, an 1882 guide to Boston Harbor. *Courtesy of the Friends of the Boston Harbor Island. Middle:* A view of Nixes Mate, then painted black, about 1909. *Courtesy of* Boston Herald. *Bottom:* A view of Nixes Mate in 2007.

long gone temple. The island's beaches are dotted with old bricks and "rip rap" and debris from the various buildings that have been on the island. A beach walk takes on the feeling of an archaeological adventure; remains of odd foundations and a gigantic tire, now filled with rocks and bricks, sit incongruously on the shore. Wharf pilings, mere sticks offshore, are the remains of a buoy depot (also called a lighthouse depot) that serviced the coast's navigational aids from about 1874 to 1921. A military switchboard room, one of several built during the 1920s to shelter military communications from attack, was once built into the side of a bluff just north of the camping area. About two years ago it collapsed, its thick walls now pancaked on the sand.

When M and I take a walk along the western shore, we hear the trilling of oystercatchers flying overhead. This is a good sign of wildlife recovery; only one to two pairs were recorded in Boston Harbor in 1989, according to a 2005 report. Crossing into the salt marsh in the island's midsection, M points out jimson weed, pepper weed and phragmites, a particularly invasive, nonnative species of reed. The red brick structure that first caught my attention is an oil shed, all that remains of the range light station. In 1902, two navigational range lights were erected here to assist mariners (range lights were also built at this time on Spectacle Island). The two light towers, one forty feet and the other thirty-one feet, were connected with a wooden walkway that also led to a six-room keeper's house, a wood shed and the oil house, according to *The Lighthouses of Massachusetts*, by Jeremy D'Entremont. In 1919, Charles Jennings, previously the keeper at Boston Light, became lighthouse keeper on Lovells. His son, Harold B. Jennings, wrote about growing up on Lovells in his 1989 book *A Lighthouse Family*. The range light burned kerosene and Harold was sometimes allowed to accompany his father when he lit the tower as darkness fell. When Harold was seven, Captain Bill Wincapaw started the tradition of the "Flying Santas"; Wincapaw (and later Edward Rowe Snow) delivered Christmas presents by plane to the remote homes of lighthouse personnel. "As a lad," Jennings wrote, "it was great to see Santa leaning out the plane door in his red suit waving a Christmas greeting, and then run after the parachuted package which would contain pencils, paper, coloring and story books, candy, gifts for the ladies and cigarettes for Dad."

The range light towers were discontinued in the late 1930s when Fort Standish was expanded. Today, they are long gone, as is the house where the Jennings once lived. Much of the area where the Jennings had a garden, raised chickens and turkeys and where young Harold played has changed; Lovells has been steadily eroding, despite a granite sea wall built in the mid-1800s on the northern tip of the island. This Ram's Head Seawall is still visible.

When I first came to Lovells in 2001, it seemed every square inch of my camping site was covered with rabbit pellets. Rabbits were everywhere, in colors ranging from midnight black to burnt sienna to dusty gray. They rustled in the bushes around the camp and skittered over the road. Climbing up the stairs of one of the batteries, I came nose to nose with one that was starting to hop down, scaring the heck out of both of us. The rabbits on Lovells are not native cottontails, however, but a domesticated breed that—naturalists speculate—were once bred on the island for meat. Some managed to escape and, being rabbits, made more rabbits, which thrived in the absence of natural predators. In the summer of 2007, however, aside from one rather tame bunny that let me creep up close enough almost to stroke its fur, I saw only a few hoppers. M, as well as a number of other park visitors and volunteers, muttered darkly about secret bunny death squads at work, but DCR officials later told me the die-off was due to a disease that cropped up from crossbreeding and overpopulation. Nature, it seems, keeps the rabbit population in balance.

On the shore nearing the northwest tip of the island, M and I cut through an archway and take a path that leads to Battery Terrill, now engulfed by a virtual jungle of plant life. After the bright light at the beach, this area is gloomy and even menacing. We peek into dark rooms of the old battery, past rusted doors and venture down stairs into total blackness. "Very *Blair Witch*," M comments adroitly. Detracting from the overall spookiness, however, is the litter and graffiti left by immature fingers.

Campers on Lovells Island are treated to a view of the huge digesters—often dubbed dinosaur eggs—of the Deer Island Sewage Treatment plant.

On the way back to the camping area, I leave M and take a path that leads from the beach up the side of the island's hill, or drumlin. Along this path is "Lovers Rock," currently a rather inconspicuous boulder. In the late nineteenth century, before the army moved the earth around it, the boulder was far more prominent and "served for many generations as a comfortable cooking place," according to James Stark in the *Illustrated History of Boston Harbor*. The rock is yet another bit of Lovells lore. In 1786, in the dead of winter, a ship from Maine wrecked on the northern side of the island, and its thirteen to fifteen passengers managed to scramble onto Lovells, taking refuge under the huge boulder. But with temperatures descending to zero, all froze to death during the night. "Two young persons, who were about to be married and who were coming to Boston to make marriage purchases, were found dead beside the rock, locked in each other's arms," Stark wrote in his 1879 book. "Few, in their hilarious moments under this benevolent boulder, ever dream of the agony of that awful night." The death of the two lovers sparked an effort by the Massachusetts Humane Society to create refuge huts on Lovells for others caught in such terrible straits—the first lifesaving facility in America.

The story of Lovers Rock may—unlike Nix and his mate—be based on fact. In December 1786, the *Massachusetts Gazette* reported that between thirteen and fifteen "unfortunates" perished on Lovells Island between December 9 and 11 after a sloop from Damariscotta "drove ashore in the last storm." The paper listed the victims; among the dead was one woman, Miss Sylvia Knap of Mansfield, identified by Snow as the doomed bride-to-be. The January 10, 1787 issue of the *Massachusetts Centinel* also reported that two of the thirteen victims "found to be missing when the other eleven were found were dug out of the snow and brought up to town." Did the deaths spark efforts to put lifesaving huts on Lovells? It's difficult to say, but according to *A History of the Boston Marine Society*, "Three representatives of the Humane Society of the Commonwealth of Massachusetts attended the 2 January 1787 meeting of the Marine Society to acquaint the members of the latter with a proposal to erect three huts on exposed beaches in or near Boston Harbor to provide shelter for shipwrecked seamen." Perhaps then, as today, it takes a tragedy to institute safety measures.

Lovells was, in fact, the scene of a number of sea disasters. The waters of Boston Harbor were tricky even for experienced sailors to navigate. Robert F. Sullivan has accounts of various sea disasters in his 1990 book, *Shipwrecks and Nautical Lore of Boston Harbor*. Sailors, he writes, said the harbor's waterways were more crooked than Boston streets, which, as any Bostonian will tell you, are crooked to the point of criminality. "Paradoxically," Sullivan writes, "a surprising number of vessels and seamen went to their destruction not on remote stretches of desolate coastline, but within plain view of the Massachusetts State House golden dome." So close and yet so far, indeed.

One of the more significant shipwrecks occurred in 1782, when the seventy-four-gun French warship, the *Magnifique*, sunk west of the northern end of Lovells with Boston pilot David Darling at the helm. The young United States government, in a fit of responsibility that has never been repeated, offered the French government the new *America*, a seventy-four-gun man-of-war being built for the U.S. Navy, as compensation. War hero John Paul Jones, who supervised the building of the *America* and had expected to captain her, was so incensed that he resigned his commission. Poor David Darling became the eighteenth-century Bill Buckner, the infamous Red Sox first baseman who let a ball go between his legs in a crucial play in the 1986 World Series. After the wreck, Darling gave up the sea to work as a sexton and undertaker and, according to James Stark, would frequently find this message from wags posted on his meetinghouse, or church, door: "Don't

A rusted door in Battery
Terrill, part of Fort Standish
on Lovells Island.

run this ship ashore/As you did the seventy-four." Sullivan, however, comes to the pilot's defense, arguing that Darling was not off course and that the ship apparently grounded during low tide and filled with water on the next high tide rather than float loose. (As for Buckner, he was forgiven in April 2008 only after two Red Sox World Series trophies.)

Attempts have been made over the years to find the *Magnifique*; some artifacts from the ship were recovered in the mid-1800s, and there are stories of buried treasure. Harold Jennings, in his book about growing up on Lovells, writes that his father dug up old coins in his garden and prints photos of the coins as proof. More recent efforts to locate the *Magnifique* have made use of the best of modern technology, including sonar and sophisticated metal-detection devices operated by researchers at the University of Massachusetts. Complicating the search are the changing borders of Lovells, which no longer resemble those seen on eighteenth- and nineteenth-century maps.

A day of rambling around Lovells can work up an appetite, even if I have been gorging on the blackberries that grow in profusion there. M has invited me to dinner. As my "covered dish," I bring politically correct couscous and cherry tomatoes; M wolfs down the cherry tomatoes but turns up his nose at the couscous. "How about a hamburger?" he says. With a well-worn spatula, M hacks off a slab of butter and slaps it into a small frying pan over a cookstove. He throws in the meat, an island in the grease, adds chopped mushrooms and cooks everything as if his life depends on charring every morsel. As the pan sizzles, we chat about the birds on the island—robins, hawks, yellow warblers, goldfinches, cedar waxwings, cardinals, woodpeckers, crows, gulls, terns, catbirds and mockingbirds. He shows me a photograph of a fox he saw on Grape Island, and we talk about the raccoons, skunks and occasional deer that inhabit the islands.

My ankles are being nibbled by insects; I think the island has decided to collect payment for all the blackberries I've been eating. To my amazement, M's hamburger tastes great, although I politely turn down seconds.

After dinner, M builds a fire below the tidal zone and we talk as the darkness gathers. We are treated to a sunset in rose and crimson that flares from behind the skyline of Boston. As the light fades, the city begins to glitter like a party girl donning her rhinestone jewelry for a night on the town. From this distance in the summer heat, Boston resembles a magical kingdom, a city of lights. There's a chorus of crickets, the crackle of the fire, the clanging of a channel bell and the sigh of the wind through the sumac. Every now and then, a plane taking off from Logan International Airport roars overhead, drowning out everything else, reminding us that we are still close to Boston's traffic and its wicked crooked streets.

1. One of the benefits of camping on Lovells Island is the view of Boston's skyline, particularly when the sun is setting.

2. Monarch butterflies on Georges Island during their fall migration.

3. A barnacle-encrusted bottle on the shore of Grape Island.

4. One of the furry inhabitants of Lovells Island.

5. The so-called "Greek Temple" is captured in this circa 1840 oil painting, titled *Rainsford's Island, Boston Harbor*, by marine artist Robert Salmon. The painting is part of the collection of the Museum of Fine Arts, Boston. The "temple" was actually a hospital. Today, nothing remains of the building but its foundation. *Image used by permission of the Museum of Fine Arts.*

6. A group campground on Lovells Island is tucked among batteries of Fort Standish.

7. Two cormorants on a dock on Thompson Island warily eyes an island visitor.

8. The collapsed walls of a former military switchboard room, which had been built into the side of a hill, remain on the shores of Lovells Island, a favorite destination for campers and kayakers.

9. Sailboats in the Boston Harbor Islands Alliance's annual sailing regatta make a loop around Little Brewster Island and Boston Light.

10. Sea glass on the shore tells a story of Spectacle's transformation from trash to treasure island.

11. One of the cottages on Peddocks Islands that once served as a café and a bordello.

12. A gazebo atop Spectacle Island.

13. *Above left:* A tunnel of trees beckons visitors to the nature preserve on the West Head of Peddocks Island.

14. *Above right:* Bumpkin attracts many groups of young campers who learn how to pack for an overnight trip.

15. A tranquil section of Deer Island in the late afternoon.

16. *Above left:* Blackberries grow in profusion on many of the Boston Harbor Islands.

17. *Above right:* All that remains of a lighthouse station on Lovells Island is the brick shell of an oil shed.

18. Sunset at Worlds End, one of the Boston Harbor Island National Park's "land" islands.

CHAPTER 6

grape island: a tale of the fox and the grapes

Foxes have an excellent sense of timing. I never realized this until a night on Grape Island, a wild gem of an island in Hingham Bay in the southern waters of the national park. Grape never underwent the kind of development found on other Harbor Islands. Hence the landscaping is a bit more "natural," giving a better sense of what the islands were like when their only human visitors were Native Americans. Author James Stark wrote in 1879 that this island had "the most beautiful woods in the Harbor," and the same holds true today. Grape is home to a variety of native and invasive species, many kinds of birds, skunks and, in recent years, foxes.

The Birdinator explained about the foxes. No, that's not his real name, and I'm not sure that this Boston Harbor Islands park ranger is aware of the nickname given to him by other rangers. But it is a moniker given with awe as well as humor; the Birdinator really knew about the feathered creatures and plants on the island. I took his early morning bird tour and pestered him until he finally took me kayaking off Grape and to nearby Slate Island. I kept asking, "What is *that*?" He seldom failed to have an answer.

The Birdinator knows about the foxes. On my first night of camping on Grape in the summer of 2007, I am dropped off by the shuttle and hump my pack into the pleasant grassy area near the dock. Grape, about fifty upland acres, lives up to its name, as there is an arbor of Concord grapes, a remnant of the time when the island was used for farming. The clearing also has chairs and picnic tables and is an excellent spot for relaxing and watching the moon rise. I pay for my campsite, chat with the rangers and then take off on the path to my right, which leads along the shoreline, which is covered with the shells of blue mussels, soft-shell clams and periwinkles. There are so many dark blue mussel shells here that one camper told me that the place should be called "Mussel Island" instead of "Grape Island." At a

A view of Grape Island and the clearing, with its grape arbor and (sometimes) its fox.

fork, I head left to pick out one of the campsites nestled in the woods along the trail. Each site has a picnic table and there are outhouses; otherwise there are no other facilities.

After setting up, I head back to the clearing by the dock to talk to the rangers. "I hear there are foxes here," I say. M, on Lovells Island, had shown me a photo of a fox he had snapped on Grape, and I was hoping to duplicate his feat. "Oh yeah. You'll see them. Every night, just about 8:00 p.m., or just about sunset, they come out here," the Birdinator tells me. Here in the clearing? Amazing! "Oh, you'll see them. No problem," he assures me.

I take off on a walk around the island; the DCR has self-guided tours printed on purple brochures. Items of interest include a midden, or waste deposit of shells and refuse left by Native Americans who made good use of Grape. A pottery shard bearing decorative imprints was found here, and author James Stark, who visited the island in the 1870s, describes finding "three stone tomahawks."

Stark also visited the Grape Island home of a salty old tar known as Captain Smith, whom he describes as an "old slaver" with the real name of Amos Pendleton. Smith was known for warning off visitors to the island

The waters of Boston Harbor are home to a huge variety of waterfowl, such as the red-breasted merganser.

with a shotgun, but Stark and a reporter from the *Boston Herald* managed to get an interview. Stark includes a lively description of the cantankerous captain, who was cajoled into telling stories about his years fighting pirates and Spanish gunboats. "As to the truth of the old slaver's statements, if anyone doubts them, we should advise such persons to visit the island, where such doubts will be quickly dispelled after an interview with Captain Smith; but if you object to hearing profane language, then keep clear of the island," Stark merrily concludes.

Captain Smith is long gone now, but the stone foundation of a farmhouse built in the early nineteenth century, which served as the caretakers' cottage, remains. One of these caretakers was Captain Billy McLeod, who, according to Edward Rowe Snow, found and tamed a baby seal. In the morning, it would take off for the ocean, returning later in the day. The seal learned to knock on the door three times with its flippers when it wanted to enter the house and slept on a rug for the night. The creature, Snow writes, died from eating green paint, and "many children who had visited the pet mourned its death." Snow added, "Captain Billy said that although he had owned many dogs since then, there never was an animal as affectionate as his little seal."

The various accounts of the Boston Harbor Islands (including, at times, this one) emphasize the human history of the islands and their place in the social and cultural history of Boston. The islands, however, are also home to a bounty of bird, animal and plant life, some native to the land and some introduced by European immigration. The famed biologist and naturalist Edward O. Wilson considers the Boston Harbor Islands a "microwilderness" and has called them "a natural laboratory seemingly made to order for research and education in biodiversity." A "Natural Resources Overview," published in May of 2005, detailed the flora and fauna found on the islands: 521 native and naturalized nonnative plants; 136 species of birds; 175 species of lichen; and 51 species of butterflies, all observed during a study from 2001 to 2003. And that's not counting the many bugs, beetles, worms and other creepy, crawling creatures, and the organisms minding their own business in tidal pools.

Grape is one of the best places to get a sense of the "wild side" of the Harbor Islands. Here, you'll find sunshine-bright yarrow, stately Queen Anne's lace and mullein with its soft, fuzzy leaves. I saw some stands of pokeberry (or pokeweed) with stems of such an intense shade of purplish pink that they looked spray painted. There is chickweed, goldenrod, jimson weed, burdock, cattails, milkweed, butter-and-eggs and pepper. Salt spray roses perfume the air when in bloom, and the hips can be nibbled for a vitamin C–packed treat. Most delightfully, on Grape you will find wild raspberry and blackberry bushes and elderberry trees. Then there are the most unwelcome invasives, such as the common reed, or *Phragmites australis*, which is dominating wetlands on the islands, and the tree of heaven, *Ailanthus altissima*, which is welcome to grow in Brooklyn but is pushing out native species in Boston Harbor.

Visitors to Grape can spend a day rambling on the well-marked grassy trails that lead around the island to various outlook points. Or they can walk around the perimeter of the island at low tide, threading their way along the rocky shore. Stepping from the beach into the land route is like walking into another dimension. One minute you're scrambling over rocks on a windy, rocky shore, the next, you are walking on a soft path in a thick wood, hearing the rustle of trees and the calls of birds. Given that the colonists seldom saw a tree they didn't want to cut down, the forests on Grape seem extraordinarily lush.

Clutching a self-guided tour brochure, I try to walk every loop of the trail. I stop to admire bushes of bayberry and various kinds of honeysuckle with red and golden berries. Catbirds call out around me; one seems very displeased with my presence and gives a *yeow* of indignation, with the injured tone my cat uses when her tail gets stepped on. Some of the once "scenic views" listed on the Grape brochure are now obscured due to the healthy tree growth.

Not so at the brochure's overlook number five. Here I sit for an hour on the convenient bench and lose myself in the vista. Below, the ocean sparkles; around me, the leaves of the aspen tremble and whisper. Boston shimmers in the distance; I see the Prudential Tower, the Federal "washboard" Building and even the Custom House Tower. I can imagine folks fuming in the traffic and the heat. A cool breeze sends the aspen leaves shimmying like Tina Turner's hem. A goldfinch flicks by. A catbird plaintively calls.

When I finally drag myself away, I press on around the island, stopping at a point that overlooks the town of Weymouth. This area was the site of a Revolutionary War–era skirmish. At one time the island was owned by a prominent Tory who invited British soldiers to gather hay on the island. Word got around that the British were on Grape, and Rebel militia decided to drive them off. Shots were exchanged, the British left and the militia landed on Grape and burned down the barn of the hapless Tory, with eighty tons of harvested hay inside. This oh-so-glorious act of agricultural destruction—the second armed confrontation of the American Revolution—has come to be called the Battle of Grape Island or the Grape Island Alarm.

I continue on a path past a group camping area and the tents of the park rangers. I finish the afternoon sampling Concord grapes and watching gulls picking up shells and dropping them from the sky in an effort to burst them open. It's easy to see how Mussel Beach was built.

At dusk, I hang out in the clearing by the pier, waiting for the fox. There is a crackle of fire; campers can make fires here as long as they are below the high-tide mark. I'm also watching for skunks. When I first camped on Grape, I was relaxing in one of the chairs, my legs comfortably up on a rest, when I noticed a skunk sniffing the air at the edge of the clearing. To my consternation, the skunk stopped, stared at me and started *running* in my direction. I had never seen a skunk run that fast; usually they are master of the you-don't-wanna-mess-with-me sort of ramble. I had no time to flee; I sat frozen in the chair, thinking that I had no way to get tomato juice, supposedly the only antidote to a skunk dousing. Mr. (or Ms.) Skunk shuffled to the base of the chair and stopped again to sniff the air. As I remained still, the skunk passed under my legs, circled the chair and finally sauntered away, going off on its own skunk business.

By the summer of 2007, there seem to be far fewer skunks; campers wonder out loud if skunk control methods have been used. Officials say the rise and fall of island animal populations is part of the cycle of nature. Deer have been seen on Grape (later I would find deer tracks) and on Bumpkin Islands; whether the creatures swim over, cross over land at low tide or walk across water frozen in winter are all possibilities.

The sun is heading toward the horizon. "Seen the fox yet?" calls the Birdinator, who is making his rounds. "Not yet," I call back. I am

A cedar waxwing is one example of the variety of bird life found on Grape Island.

prepared. My headlamp flashlight is affixed to my brow, and my camera is at the ready.

Kids from a group campsite race by. They are part of an extended family who lives in Hingham and spends a week on the island every summer, coming by their own boat. Grape Island was, they joked, their summer house. "We're like the Beverly Hillbillies, with all this stuff," one of the women explained. A boy has a box filled with water and tiny crabs he's gathered. "What are you going to do with them?" I ask. "Hang out with them and put them back tomorrow," he says. (Which he does, minus a few that managed to escape overnight.)

It's getting darker. "See the fox yet?" the ranger asks (this is getting annoying) as he heads for his tent for the night. "Not yet," I say. Would I be the only one on Grape *not* to see the fox? I wait as night descends. Soon it is too dark to make out anything in the clearing. Resigned to a foxless night, I switch on my headlamp and prepare to leave when the beam picks up two eyes, close together and close to the ground. The fox! I move toward the eyes, and they wink out. I stop and move again slowly. The eyes again! But again they disappear. I wait. I see nothing. I give up and head toward my tent. As I walk along the path, I stop to admire the light from a campfire on the shore. A family is hunkered around the flames with all the accoutrements, including sizzling marshmallows on sticks. The fire lights up their faces, ruddy with the joy of togetherness. As I admire their animation, I realize I'm not the only one outside the circle watching them. My headlamp picks up the reflection

The elusive fox on Grape Island. *Courtesy of the Boston Harbor Islands Conservation Society, www. bhics.com, copyright 2006–2008 Michael C. Madej.*

of eyes in the bushes near the fire. I move in with my camera, stumbling in the brush, hoping the flash will pick up the fox's body in a photo. The eyes disappear and reappear some feet away. I awkwardly move toward the eyes, and the eyes move again. For about twenty minutes, I follow those fox eyes; the creature would move away from the fire, going around in circles that led back to the outskirts of the fire every time. The Birdinator would later tell me foxes are fascinated by fire. I never got off a camera shot. Not once did I glimpse the body; only the eyes. The fox's timing and judgment of distance were impeccable. I finally leave off the chase and go to bed.

The next morning the Birdinator takes me around the island on a bird-watching walk, something offered to island visitors when time and expertise permit. We see wrens, woodpeckers, chickadees, goldfinches and an Eastern Phoebe that gets the Birdinator very excited, as it is rare. He shows me how to identify the staghorn sumac by rubbing its soft, furry stems, which resemble a buck's velvety antlers. You can make a drink called "Sumac-ade" from the pink fruit, he says. Actually it's pretty wretched stuff, he admits, but you can drink it safely. He picks wild black cherries, which are delicious. "Just don't eat the seeds. They have cyanide," he says, as I almost choke. He also points out a stand of the island's chief bully, the invasive tree of heaven. He shows me elderberries, which have a strange, sweet flavor.

"Do you know how to call in birds?" he asks. "You make a wwwwuuusssss sound. The sound attracts birds. No one knows why. WWWWWUSSSSSS," he calls. Indeed, the birds seem to respond to his call. I try to imitate it, but I can't quite get it, and the birds flee in terror.

The DCR, hoping to start a program for kayak rentals on the islands, provided kayaks in the summer of 2007 as a pilot. The Birdinator takes me out on a kayak into Hingham Harbor toward Slate Island, a low, long isle where slate was once mined. "From this island came the slate that covered the roofs of many famous homes and meeting places in New England," declared Patrick Connelly in 1932's *Islands of Boston Harbor*. And like always, New Englanders didn't know where to stop; slate was nearly decimated. However, the demand for the rock eventually slacked off, and the island remains. Kayaking gives a visitor yet another perspective on these islands; being rocked by the waves gives a more intimate relationship with the water. You also get a sense of the harbor as a thoroughfare. We often had to wait for large boats—commercial and private—to pass by.

That night, I wait for the fox in the clearing. And right after sunset, just as the light grows dim, he or she appears. I get a good look at the long, low body and bushy tail and snap a blurry photo of something that looks like the Loch Ness fox. Even if I don't get a good photo, the sighting is successful. The eight o'clock fox knows the schedule.

CHAPTER 7

bumpkin island: curing body and spirit

Tuesday, July 24, 6:45 p.m.
This is an exquisite time of day. The air's cooling off, the light is soft, diffuse, due to the haze. Even the wind is getting softer. I'm completely alone, yet I'm in full sight of civilization. Only a quarter mile of ocean separates me from someone's front door, someone's back yard. Yet I might as well be hundreds of miles away.

Tide is going out on its perpetual seesaw. Mentally, I'm still in Boston. I continue to be bothered by the garbage I picked up on the beach today, the (used) toilet paper that was on the edge of my campsite. Why are we humans given such beauty only to spoil it? Do people not know? Not care?

There are lovely wildflowers on this island—yellows, purples, white. And it's lovely to have campsites so near the ocean. Especially mine, which is tucked into the trees fronting on a postcard vista.

When you stay overnight in a place, you notice more. You're not rushing to make the last ferry or worried about the tides and getting back to your boat in time. You can sit on the beach and ponder the shape and textures of rocks and shells, the shimmering iridescence on the shore. How the wind shifts—a hot breath, then a cool sigh.

I can see a large sightseeing boat in the distance, its passengers on deck taking in the views. But on a boat, can you get the sense of the sea and the sweet smell of grass, or does everything rush by too fast in a throbbing surge of speed and foam? How soft the wind is now.

I wrote that in 2001, on my first night on Bumpkin Island—indeed, the first night of my very first day ever on the Boston Harbor Islands. I ran across the description in an old notebook, scribbled between quotes from interviews with other campers and rangers and a "note to self" to complain about the Reserve America system that had erroneously listed me as camping on Grape, not Bumpkin. Much has changed since that first visit

The remains of a military mess hall still stand on Bumpkin Island, although it is now filled with poison ivy.

to the islands, and yet very little has changed. Bumpkin is still an oasis of peace and calm, garbage is still a problem and the Reserve America system has its glitches.

Bumpkin, with its thirty-five upland acres, is an ideal spot to get introduced to what camping on a Harbor Island is all about. There's no running water or electricity, but there are outhouses and about a dozen campsites; some of them are nestled among staghorn sumac and elderberry trees along the beach on the southern side, the rest are set among the forested area on the higher ground of the island's interior. Bumpkin is also a spectacular spot for a day trip, with numerous picnic sites and great beaches for exploring. There are also a number of historical sites on the island that underscore with poignancy the history of the islands as a place of refuge and retreat.

Landing at the dock of the island, the first building you notice is the stone hut that now serves as quarters for the rangers. It seems perched at the side of a hill; the rise of Bumpkin dramatically illustrates the concept of "drumlin." Not surprisingly, the dome-like Bumpkin was also called Round Island (as well as Bomkin Island and Pumpkin Island). The paths that go to the left and right of the dock rise steeply—the island reaches a height of seventy feet—and you can either head for the large picnic area in a clearing (to the left) or go to the right toward the camping spots. Paths circle and cross the island, so even if you don't grab a map/brochure at the entrance, it's hard to get lost (although many kids have tried over the years).

Park ranger Eva Van Aken takes visitors on a tour of Bumpkin Island's edible and/or useable plants during the summer of 2007.

Once part of the town of Weymouth, Bumpkin was later bequeathed to Harvard College, which leased it to tenant farmers who grew fruits and vegetables and harvested hay. Thus, the growth you see is not original; Bumpkin, like many of the islands, lost most of its trees to land-clearing practices. Photographs taken about 1900 show an island totally stripped of trees, with one large, imposing building sitting on the highest point of the island. This building was once a monument to both compassion and conspicuous consumption.

The history of Bumpkin Island is closely linked with the name of millionaire businessman and omnivorous intellectual Albert Cameron Burrage. Sometimes dubbed the Copper King, Burrage (1859–1931) was a well-rounded Boston Brahmin who dabbled in politics, philanthropy, geology and botany even while piling up riches and lavishing his home and family with the best that money could buy. The scion of an old New England family, Burrage grew up in California and later graduated from Harvard in 1883, ranking twenty-second in his class. He studied law, and began practicing in Boston in 1884. He was briefly on the Boston Transit Commission, which built the nation's first subway, and he also ran several Boston gas companies. As a member of the Boston Common Council, he introduced the "Burrage Ordinance" in 1892, which was to prevent city employees from presiding at any political caucus. "This important measure has severely wrung the withers of the party hacks, and efforts are being made to bring about its repeal," Burrage proudly informed his fellow Harvard classmates in an anniversary publication about the class of 1883.

In 1898, Burrage resigned from his gas company positions to pursue the production of low-grade copper ore. He helped found Amalgamated Copper and later the Chile Copper Company, ventures that apparently made him fabulously wealthy. He displayed that wealth to Boston when he built an extravagant mansion in the French chateau style at 314 Commonwealth Avenue in 1901. The Burrage Mansion—which still stands—was replete with architectural flourishes and was furnished with marble, carved oak and a "number of elegantly finished bathrooms," according to a gushing article in the *Boston Globe* on September 28, 1902. "Magnificent as is this private palace, Mr. Burrage, who is many times a millionaire, spends only a portion of his time in it, for he owns not only a beautiful summer place at Cohasset but also has a costly and castle-like residence in Redlands, Calif.," the article noted. Some critics, however, sniffed that the Boston mansion was too gaudy for good taste.

Perhaps Burrage, or his wife, decided that there were other outlets for his wealth. About 1900, the Burrages decided to fund a hospital for disabled or infirm children in a place where the little ones could breathe healthy salt air, enjoy the sunshine and play in a safe, compassionate environment. Burrage leased Bumpkin Island, then described as a "treeless, dreary-looking mound," from his alma mater Harvard (for one hundred or five hundred years, depending on different newspapers accounts) and built a hospital, painted bright yellow, on its highest point. The Burrage Hospital for Crippled Children opened in July of 1902, when the first "boatload of sick, crippled and deformed children was transferred from the hot, stifling city to the cool and pleasant wards of the hospital on Bumpkin Island," reported the *Globe* on July 15, 1902. No expense was spared in building the spacious, three-story facility, which had running water and its own gas plant. Charles Brigham, who designed Burrage's Commonwealth Avenue mansion, also designed the hospital. Newspaper scribes were particularly

A weatherworn copy of a photograph of philanthropist Albert C. Burrage greets visitors from its position on the dock of Bumpkin Island. Burrage once funded a crippled children's hospital on the island.

intrigued by "an inclined runway that leads from floor to floor, a half flight at a time." Mrs. Burrage had seen this "peculiar feature" in California and brought it to Bumpkin. Today, few would marvel at a handicap ramp in a hospital.

Perhaps the hospital was built as a monument to Burrage's community spirit or his ego, or perhaps it was his wife's pet project, but that mattered little to the 140 or so children, suffering from heart or other physical conditions, who were provided with free care during the summer. Doctors said another goal was happiness. "Play," a doctor told a Globe reporter, "when the child is not overdoing it, is a prime factor in working a cure."

Visitors today may puzzle over why a children's hospital was located so far from the city, with its conveniences and professional services. Was the Burrage Hospital another example of the practice of placing institutions deemed unsuitable for city life out on the island? Let us remember, nineteenth- and early twentieth-century sentiments held that fresh air, particularly sea air, had healing properties. Throughout the early 1900s, hundreds of children in Boston were taken to the Harbor Islands (including Bumpkin) on free outings; there they were provided with food and, in many cases, even bathing suits, as an antidote to crushing urban poverty. Those of us of a certain age can remember how in the classic book *Little Women*, set in the nearby Massachusetts city of Concord, Jo's dearest wish was to bring her ailing sister Beth to the seashore for a cure. Beth does, indeed, feel better after the sojourn, although she succumbs romantically by the end of the novel. But you get the point.

Unfortunately for the little Beths of Boston, war intervened. During World War I, Burrage transferred his island lease to the federal government and, beginning in 1917, the Bumpkin Hospital was used by the U.S. Navy for housing its sailors. The military also built as many as fifty-eight buildings that held more than 1,300 sailors at one time on the island, according to Edward Rowe Snow. Burrage also gave the military use of his steam-powered yacht, the *Aztec*, described as a 260-foot "floating palace" in the *Globe*.

After the armistice, most of the buildings on Bumpkin were torn down or moved, and after a brief reopening in the 1940s, the children's hospital stood empty. In 1945, a fire gutted the building. For years, its ruins dominated the island's landscape, with the roofless walls jutting out at the island's highest point, until these finally collapsed.

Burrage went on to other things, including suing the government for the condition of the *Aztec* when it was returned. He became an obsessive collector of minerals and rocks and he also was well known as a horticulturalist, particularly of orchids. Burrage served as a president of the

A land bridge forms from Bumpkin Island to Hull during low tide.

Bumpkin is a popular island for camping excursions and a good way to teach young hikers how to pack light.

Massachusetts Horticultural Society and of the American Orchid Society; his *Burrage on Vegetables* book is considered a classic. Strangely, he may have considered the Burrage Hospital one of his failures; he never mentions it in his updates to his Harvard classmates. He died in 1931 and left his large mineral collection, including some spectacular gold specimens, to Harvard. The Burrage mansion on Commonwealth Avenue remained in the family until 1947, when his widow died. Today it has been converted into condominiums.

Over the years, the walls of the Burrage children's hospital have tumbled down. Today, all that remains are heaps of yellow and red bricks, choked with poison ivy. One of the navy buildings has fared better. You can still peek into what's left of the Naval Training Station's mess hall, a rather imposing ruin, if also filled with poison ivy. Just a few yards away is a stone building thought to date back to the 1800s. First used as a home, it later became a heating plant for the hospital. The rough stones, called beach cobbles, have a patina of striking yellow lichen, perhaps a tribute to the bright yellow bricks of the long-gone children's hospital. The stone building near the dock, which now provides shelter to rangers, was once used as a pump station to supply salt water to the island's fire hydrants.

Bumpkin abounds with natural features; the human impact on the island has been softened by time. There are trails, some following the remains of roads, which crisscross the island and lead to scenic views. On the northern side, you can see downtown Boston, eight miles away, and get view of Peddocks, Hull and, in the distance, Great Brewster. Tours of useful or edible plant life on the island are often offered by the rangers. There are bayberry bushes, salt spray roses (a nonnative import from China), dewberries, milkweed, bull thistle and hackberry. Chances are rangers will tell you that the fuzzy red berries of the staghorn sumac can be used to make Sumac-ade, as the Birdinator once told me. Chances are they will also add that it tastes pretty bad. (Which makes me wonder why everyone mentions it.)

Depending on the time of your trip, you may experience one of the most magical features of a Bumpkin stay: the formation of a land bridge from the island to the mainland of Hull. Depending on the tide, a spit of land rises from the island's southern edge, like something out of a Harry Potter adventure, albeit at a natural rate of progression, not the instant gratification of magic. If you keep close track of the time, you can walk to the Hull shore and back, finding curious stones and sea life and spooking the birds that use the bridge as a landing zone.

A trip to Bumpkin may not cure everything that ails you, but it does restore your spirits.

CHAPTER 8

the challenge
of peddocks island

From the shell of an old fort, a conference center complex has been created for groups and individuals seeking an island getaway close to home. They come for meetings and retreats from urban life, and they come partly because they know that this development is constantly seeking better techniques for making use of the earth's materials with minimal depletion; sustainable technology is the shorthand.
–A description of a possible future for Peddocks Island, excerpted from the Boston Harbor Islands 2003 General Master Plan, issued by the Boston Harbor Islands Partnership

Y ou know," said the ranger as he led me under the canopy of trees that has engulfed Fort Andrews on Peddocks Island, "you could film a whole movie on this island and not know it was an island." What a movie it could be! It would be flush with the mystery and intrigue of a crumbling turn-of-the-century fort; it would have breathtaking close-ups of sun-dappled forests and open meadows; and it would be filled with historical drama among the cottages of "Crab Alley," a small community where Portuguese fishermen once lived.

With five drumlins, Peddocks is among the largest of the Harbor Islands. Its 210 upland acres encompass a wide range of terrains, including woodlands, beaches, meadows and salt ponds. You can spend hours rambling from its East Head to its West Head, something to keep in mind when you're trying to get back to the pier in time for the inter-island shuttle. In some ways, Peddocks can be considered an archipelago; three of its five drumlins are connected only by lowland or sand spits, giving the impression of being three separate islands. More so on Peddocks than on any of the other islands, you get a sense of what it was once like to live year-round in Boston Harbor. Almost all the buildings on Bumpkin and Lovells have entirely disappeared. Not so on Peddocks. Inside the Endicott-era Fort

A fire-gutted barracks of Fort Andrews on Peddocks Island is one of the fort's structures that is likely destined for demolition.

Andrews, officers' quarters, barracks and other structures that once bustled with soldiers and prisoners of war still stand. The small cottages dotting the Middle Head of the island speak eloquently of fishermen and their descendants who resided on the island and made a living from the sea. The marshes and thickly wooded areas on the West Head give visitors a sense of the time before those tree-chopping Europeans arrived, the centuries when native people fished and foraged along Peddocks's shores.

With all its allure and potential as a Harbor Island destination, there's a bittersweet melancholy about Peddocks. Fort Andrews, despite a huge number of surveys and studies, continues to deteriorate; with each year, a bit more of what could be preserved diminishes. While some people—a few full time—continue to live on the island, their self-reliant way of life seems at odds with the twenty-first century, and their privately owned homes clash with the concept of a public park. "The island has become its own living ghost [with] memories of days of yore," as Matilda Silvia writes in her memoir of growing up on Peddocks, *Once Upon an Island*. Peddocks is the Boston Harbor Island with the greatest amount of living history, and thus for the Boston Harbor Islands Partnership, the island's future remains one of its greatest challenges.

The archaeological record suggests that Native Americans often traversed the drumlins of what is now Peddocks; a skull more than four thousand years old was found there in 1971. The island has been placed on the National Register of Historic Places in recognition of its archaeological significance. What was later called Peddocks Island was settled in 1634 by Puritans; by 1844, most of the land was owned by various farmers. The island is named after an English planter named Leonard Peddock, although the island's spelling wandered in that quaint seventeenth-century way from "Pettick's" to "Paddock's" and even to "Petix." During the American Revolution, Peddocks was the scene of skirmishes, mainly over livestock, between British and revolutionary forces. In the early 1800s, the bluffs of the island's Prince Head, a narrow drumlin connected by a very narrow strip of land to the main island, served as a target for the shells of artillery manufactured on Nut Island. (Nut Island is now connected to the Hough's Neck area of Quincy.)

Long before the Boston Harbor Islands National Park was created, Peddocks Island was a place for recreation, although not always the most savory kind. Two inns were established on the island: the Y.O. West End House, owned by William Drake, and the Island Hotel, run by John Irwin. A surviving menu from the Island Hotel café showed it offered a full range of food and drink. A sarsaparilla was ten cents, a Budweiser was twenty-five cents and a gin fizz was twenty. Broiled live lobster would set you back a whole seventy-five cents, and boiled tripe would take forty cents out of your pocket. The Island Hotel, however, often served more than food to those willing to pay the price. A small cottage near the hotel was used as a café and its two small bedrooms provided female companionship for a price; money was slipped into a slot under a window. In 1909, the Boston newspapers were filled with stories about so-called "Chinese picnics" and subsequent police raids on Peddocks. ("Chinese picnic" was a euphemism for a gathering where people used opium.) Additionally, both Drake and Irwin were prosecuted for illegal gambling and liquor sales; ironically, according to a reference I found in the *Boston Globe*, Drake was (or became) a member of the Boston police and the state police.

Peddocks attracted those looking to skirt other laws. The Boston Braves made an end run around the blue laws prohibiting baseball action in Boston on Sundays by playing on Peddocks. Peddocks was also the site of hard-fought battles between local baseball teams and many an "old-timers" game. A baseball player and fan himself, Irwin sponsored many of these games. (Irwin seemed to be from a baseball-loving family; according to a 1920 *Boston Globe* article, his brother was a scout for the New York Yankees.)

Life on the island, while charming in the summer, turned harsh during the long New England winters. Nevertheless, Portuguese fishermen settled along the shores of Peddocks in the 1880s, a number of them from Long Island. When Boston decided to expand hospitals and other facilities on

The Island Hotel on Peddocks Island once offered a full range of food and drink. *Courtesy of Shelia Martel.*

Long Island, a group of the Portuguese fishermen who had lived there for decades were told to leave. Some resettled on Middle Brewster and Great Brewster, but others loaded their small shacks on boats or barges and floated them to the East Head of Peddocks. Here, they established another fishing community, paying a yearly fee to the island's private owners, then the Andrews family, for the right to live in their shanties. A *Boston Globe* article dated August 22, 1909, describes a "quaint village" on the island's western shore consisting of neat houses with tiny gardens sheltering "families whose heads make a living by catching fish and lobster." The article urged readers to visit the "picturesque" location, adding, "There is no style put on in the Peddocks fishing village but the folks who live there appear to enjoy themselves and abide in comfort."

As early as 1892, Boston considered buying Peddocks as a recreational site, but in the late 1890s, the U.S. Army decided to include Peddocks in the government's Endicott plan for coastal defense. In keeping with the philosophy of spreading out defense systems, the army built batteries, gun positions and support facilities throughout the two drumlins of East Head, which strategically overlook the harbor's Nantasket Roads channel. Work began in 1897 and continued through the early twentieth century. Fort Andrews—named for George Leonard Andrews, major general of volunteers for the U.S. Army during the Civil War—became a sprawling complex of batteries, bunkers and barracks, with its own firehouse, warehouse, bakery and mess hall. In May of 1904, Colonel C.S. Vestal took command of Fort Andrews.

Once again the Portuguese fishermen who lived in cottages on East Head were forced to move, this time in deference to the U.S. military. A number of their cottages were floated to the island's Middle Head; the area has been called Portuguese Cove since then. Indeed, transporting homes by water seemed to be a custom in Boston Harbor. In her memoir of growing up on Peddocks, Matilda Silvia tells of how, in 1910, her father, Alexander Bies, a tailor for Fort Andrews, decided to move his house in deference to his new bride, who didn't want to live so close to the military complex. The house was jacked up and loaded on a floating platform. The home was almost to its new location on the west side of East Head when it started to sink and it ended up stranded in several feet of water on the beach, minus its chimney, an event covered with great merriment by the *Boston Traveler*. ("Looking like some sort of new warship, the house of Alexander Bees [*sic*] of Peddock's Island made a disastrous trip around the island today.") Army mules finally dragged the home to its final resting place. Silvia would grow up in that home.

Fort Andrews, like the other forts on the harbor, never saw action. During World War I, several artillery companies trained here before shipping overseas. During the 1920s, the fort reverted to caretaker status; it was reactivated in 1940 and served as the regimental headquarters for the 241st Coast Artillery Corps. During World War II, Boston Harbor was considered a potential target for enemy submarines and ships. All pleasure craft were banned from the harbor. Bob Enos, whose grandfather built a summer cottage on the island in the early 1900s, remembers getting to the island by government boat when the family spent summers there in the 1940s. Submarine nets were installed across Hull Gut, the area between Peddocks and Hull, and across West Gut, between Peddocks and Nut Island. (Traces of the west net can reportedly still be seen at low tide.) Tall tales have been told about German U-boats that allegedly snuck into—and perhaps even sank in—Boston Harbor.

The military and civilian sides of Peddocks were clearly demarcated. Soldiers were known to slip over to the civilian side for the homemade hooch and other amenities offered by locals and in the island's hotels. Silvia once recited a poem as recorded by Bob Enos about the potent qualities of the rum available in "Spickville," the very politically incorrect term for villagers who could not "speak" English:

> *If you ever come down to Fort Andrews*
> *And you want to get in with the bunch*
> *You better come down quite early*
> *And don't forget your lunch.*

The poem goes on to describe rum as being "better for cuts and bruises, better than iodine." And then:

> *If you ever wake up in the morning*
> *and your head is full of pain,*
> *just take a drink of the village rum*
> *and you'll never wake up again.*

The army was, perhaps, not displeased when Drake's hotel burned down in 1913 and Irwin's hotel was shuttered.

Families on Middle Head also visited the fort; Sheila Martel, the fifth generation of a family descended from the original Portuguese villagers, remembers her mother and father heading over to the fort on Saturday night for a meal of frank and beans and a movie. Claire Hale, whose family has summered on the island since 1919, remembers how as a kid she and other island children would watch cartoons in one of the fort's mess halls. On Sundays, villagers walked to a small wooden chapel, which had been

Many of the twenty-six remaining structures of Fort Andrews on Peddocks Island retain a sense of past glory, even if some are now past repair. This building, used to house officers, was built between 1904 and 1906 on what is now called "Officers' Row."

built by the army in the 1940s on the island's northeast side, for Sunday services. The chapel has a particularly poignant place in the memory of the villagers.

During World War II, about 1,800 Italian prisoners of war were housed on Peddocks. It was not a hardship assignment; while the prisoners had war work assignments in Boston, they were allowed to grow vegetables on the island and cook their own Italian-style meals. They were often visited by Italian Americans living in the Boston area. Claire Hale, who is of Italian descent, remembers having the prisoners over for dinner in her family's cottage, and everyone eating huge portions of macaroni and lobster as the prisoners chatted in Italian with her grandmother.

The Italian prisoners also worshipped at the fort chapel. "The Italian prisoners had a choir," Bob Enos recalled. "I think there was a choir master from Pemberton who would come over to work with them. It was glorious; it was like going to La Scala. It was just unbelievably beautiful singing." Many of the prisoners, too, have warm memories of their time on the island. In 2001, one of those former prisoners, Luigi DiGiorgio, a tank driver captured in North Africa, returned to the island for a visit, telling a *Boston Globe* reporter it was a "a great joy" to return to the place where he had spent thirty pleasant months. Observers described watching the eighty-

World War II Italian prisoners of war found that their "incarceration" on Peddocks Island had many benefits, including getting to know some of the local young women. *Courtesy of Claire Hale.*

year-old DiGiorgio drop to his knees and kiss the ground. In the summer of 2007, while riding the inter-island shuttle, I met an elderly woman visiting Peddocks for the first time in more than sixty years who was flooded with memories of how she had come out to Peddocks as a child with her mother to bring food to the Italian prisoners. Reportedly, as many as fifty prisoners ended up marrying women from Boston's Italian American neighborhood in the city's North End.

After World War II, the fort was again relegated to caretaker status, and in 1958 the fort area was sold as government surplus to a private company, which then bought the rest of the island as well, with the aim of developing it for residential real estate. The development, however, never got off the ground. Cottage owners—some of them descendants from the original Portuguese fishermen and some of them Boston-area residents who had bought and improved the original shacks—continued to live on the island or spend summers there. The cottage owners never actually owned any land on the island, not even the land beneath their houses. They owned only their homes. Over the years they had paid user fees to the island's owners. In 1970 the state's Metropolitan District Commission (MDC) acquired the island, which became part of the Boston Harbor Island State Park and subsequently the Boston Harbor Islands National Park Area. The island remains the property of the state's Department of Recreation and Conservation, which replaced the MDC in 2004.

A trip to Peddocks Island by water shuttle begins at a modern pier, built in 2000. At the end of the pier, there is a visitors' center established in a 1910 guardhouse. Here you can see old photos of Fort Andrews, when its proud, new buildings stood on hilltops shorn of trees, and practice rounds were fired from its batteries. Other exhibits describe the island's animal and plant life. Behind the guardhouse is the former stable, now used to house the park rangers who stay on the island during the summer. Here, also, are public outhouses.

Nearby the visitors' center, along the shore, is the wooden chapel where islanders and Italian prisoners once worshiped together more than sixty years ago. The chapel was badly in need of repair in the summer of 2007; the interior had been damaged by vandals, and it remains closed to the public. Near the parade grounds rises the dramatic brick shell of a former barracks, gutted by fire. Minus its roof, the structure is now nearly engulfed in vegetation. From here an old road, past several still-standing barracks, leads into the interior of the fort. Old photos of the fort in its prime hardly prepare you for the overgrown ghostly appearance of the various structures now. Many of the buildings are tumbling down, their insides exposed to reveal plumbing and insulation. Others have been boarded up or plastered with signs screaming "danger" or warning of asbestos. The batteries are crumbling, and there are gloomy, dark corridors smelling of water rot. Yet an overall sense of past glory lingers. The fort was built at a time of growing American military might; Fort Andrews was a showpiece of strength as well as a strategic fortification. As one ranger told me, "They were building forts to be impressive. The United States was emerging as a world power. You can't help but walk the island and be amazed." Claire Hale and her husband Bill, who still own a cottage on the island, remember the beautiful floors and tiled fireplaces of the fort's officers' quarters, the warming ovens built into

A chapel on Peddocks Island built by the army in the 1940s was once a place of worship for soldiers, islanders and World War II Italian prisoners of war.

the radiators, the china cabinets in the quarters and dramatic staircases. Many of the structures have front porches, a luxury in a military zone.

As a brochure from the DCR states, "Nowhere else in Boston Harbor does an Endicott-period military reservation retain such a large percentage of the original structures that house and supported its peacetime garrison. Usually, if anything survives, it tends to be only a fort's concrete gun batteries." Three of the fort's four brick barracks remain; the fourth was destroyed in a fire. The wooden barracks have disappeared. Remaining structures—in various stages of disrepair—include the post's bakery and canteen, firehouse, hospital, gym, a large storehouse, noncommissioned officers' quarters, commanding officers' quarters, officers' quarters and bachelor officers' quarters. Tucked among the ruins are seemingly incongruous red fire hydrants, their crimson paint defying the passage of time. The once-majestic views are obscured by thick tree growth, and the ground is choked with poison ivy; there is even a stand of kudzu—an invasive plant that is the scourge of the South—which may have been planted by the army for erosion control.

Any description of Fort Andrews requires one major caveat: the entire fort area was fenced off and closed to the general public in 2005. Decaying buildings were deemed a hazard to visitors who insisted on climbing through the structures, endangering themselves and the buildings. Rangers are sometimes able to give tours of the fort, depending on staffing levels and other considerations. The fort, however, is officially off limits.

If you follow the path on the southern side of the island that skirts the fort, you cross a long sand spit called a "tombolo" that leads to the island's Middle Head. A row of cottages bisecting the highest point of the drumlin is known as Crab Alley, a place where Portuguese fishermen once sold their wares in sheds near their homes. On the shore nearby is a house-sized boulder dubbed Pudding Rock, which has emerged from the Middle Head bluff as the shore eroded; it is covered with graffiti, in large part the names of island children.

Crossing over Middle Head, you pass a salt pond and plunge into the thickly wooded area of West Head, which is now a nature preserve. Walking through a tunnel of trees, you can quickly forget you're near a former war fortification and feel instead as though you've returned to the time when Native Americans visited the Harbor Islands. The path leads to a freshwater, if brackish, pond on the eastern shore. You can walk along the beach here (which, unfortunately, collects a lot of trash from boat traffic) and you can also circumnavigate Prince Head (depending on the tides). Keep an eye out: birds seen on the island include the redwing blackbird, cedar waxwing, black-crowned night heron, barn swallow, gray catbird and goldfinch.

On your way back, you may want to explore more of Middle Head, which is dotted with about forty cottages, many of them neat and well maintained. Some of the fishermen's cottages originally floated over from Long Island and then relocated to Middle Head are still standing here, set along a bluff overlooking Quincy Bay. The brightly painted "Pink House" is a landmark, marking the beginning of Crab Alley. The section got its name in the previous century: "The fisherman had sheds on one side of the trail and their cottages on the other, and they sold fish from the little sheds. Hence the name Crab Alley," said Suzanne Gall Marsh, founder of Friends of the Boston Harbor Islands and a cottage owner. A small general store was once operated on Crab Alley; it is long gone. Enos, an artist who did a research and art project on Peddocks for a 1986 master's thesis, described the original houses:

> *One-story, cellarless houses with three or four fairly small rooms. The ceilings were low, like a ship's cabin, which made them easy to heat in the winter. A big iron stove occupied the middle of the living room. There*

Massachusetts artist and teacher Bob Enos spent his summers as a youth on Peddocks
Island in a cottage built by his father. He did his 1986 master's thesis on island life,
which included research and numerous sketches of cottages that were once the homes of
Portuguese fishermen and their families. He is holding one of those sketches.

*was a table and chairs with a kerosene lamp and usually a portable radio.
The beds filled the small bedrooms, with the clothes hung from hooks in
the wall.*

Over the years these simple shacks have been improved and added to
as the working fishermen gradually gave way to those seeking a summer
retreat. Today, none of the houses in the alley has running water or
electricity, although some have wells, so owners display creative engineering;
one owner has even devised a hot water system using dark-colored hoses.

Peddocks residents tell many stories of island life. They talk about Mabel
Pinto, the so-called "Mayor of Peddocks Island," a woman who came to the
island in 1918 as a bride of a fisherman and who was considered the best
crab picker on the island. "She could pick twelve crabs in fifteen minutes,
which produced one pound of crabmeat and sold in the 1930s and 1940s

for one dollar," Enos said. The islanders talk of the island caretaker's beloved dog Dante, a huge, friendly canine that would stop children from venturing too far out in the harbor waters. Dante's grave, with paw prints on its marker, sits on a bluff overlooking the shore, and kids still leave balls and flowers beside it. Around Labor Day every year, islanders hold "Kids Day," complete with old-fashioned egg tosses and sack races, although the number of kids participating decreases every year. Shelia Martel told me, only half joking, that she was not allowed to date anyone who didn't like island life, since summers on the island were the lifeblood of her family. Similarly, Silvia writes in her memoir, "The island was always part of my life, one I was never willing to give up, even for work, or marriage."

Among the well-kept cottages, however, there are others in bad shape. A number are without doors or windows and are falling apart; some seem to be little more than piles of lumber and debris. At least one of them was marked with a handmade sign in the summer of 2007 that read: "Property of the DCR." Herein lies a dilemma of Peddocks: What to do about private ownership in a public park?

Many believe that the cottage dwellers should not be there at all, and since 1970 there have been numerous efforts by the Commonwealth's Metropolitan District Commission to expel them. Certainly the cottages predate both the state and national park. Yet their owners do not and never have actually owned the land beneath them; they have only owned the houses

Some of the cottages on Peddocks Island that owners say were originally floated here from Long Island by Portuguese fishermen.

themselves. For years they have paid a yearly permit fee, first to the island's private owners and then to the MDC. When the state park was created in the 1970s, the cottage dwellers were given ten years to vacate, according to Bill Hale, today a member of the park's advisory board. However, the deadline passed without any action taken by the MDC. In 1992 a compromise was worked out: the current owners would be allowed to remain in their cottages until they died; they would not be allowed to pass on the cottages to their children or sell them to anyone else, however. On their death, the cottages would become the property of the MDC. Cottage owners now wonder if the compromise dooms a vital part of Peddocks history. Over the years, they have watched as cottages owners died or left and their deserted homes were taken over by the MDC. Until recently, when the MDC took over a cottage, its doors and windows would be removed to prevent squatting, and the structure would slowly succumb to the forces of time. In July of 2001, about seven deserted cottages were demolished under the personal supervision of the MDC commissioner, over the fierce objections of other cottage owners.

For those who see the cottages, particularly those in Crab Alley, as historically important, such destruction is a travesty. "It breaks my heart to see some of their cottages today," Marsh told me. "There's a history for each one of those buildings."

Today, the DCR, which has replaced the MDC, and other park officials are attempting to determine which of the cottages can be saved and what to do about them. Some of the current cottage owners say they would like to be able to pass on their cottages to family members, insisting that occupied cottages add value to the park. Owners mow the grass, maintain the walkways, clean up litter and serve as eyes and ears during the high tourist season at a time when there may be as few as one or two park rangers on the island. Many say they are willing to put up with the curious stares of island visitors, as long as the public is generally respectful and mindful of their privacy. (Although not all islanders have always acted this way, I'm told.) Claire Hale, however, is very happy to talk to visitors. "Ask questions of the cottagers; they'll talk to you," she said. Island life and what it represents "is too priceless to let go," said Judy McDevitt, who came to the island in 1961 as the wife of the caretaker and has lived there since.

Other visitors may view the cottage owners as unfairly getting a sweet deal on parkland. Many, including officials and volunteers, say that while they are sympathetic to the cottage owners, this kind of private ownership simply is not compatible with the goals of a national park. The cottage owners, for their part, look at the decay of Fort Andrews and shake their heads. Why should they relinquish control of the cottages only to watch them, too, fall apart? Still, over the years a few islanders have shown little regard for cottage history. Many of the abandoned cottages are filled with trash, such as empty propane tanks, broken furniture and even an old refrigerator; others have been ransacked for wood or other material.

So what does the future hold for Peddocks? Will the public ever get to walk through Fort Andrews unimpeded? Many of the buildings in Fort Andrews may be doomed; they may need to be torn down and removed for safety's sake. Other buildings, however, can be salvaged and still others may be preserved as historical ruins. The park administration is currently trying to determine which those are. Complicating the process is the fact that, as every year goes by, the balance tilts further in the direction of demolition.

The Boston Harbor Islands Partnership does, in fact, have a vision for Peddocks. In its 2003 comprehensive General Master Plan for all the Harbor Islands, the partnership envisions building a family all-inclusive "eco-camp" on Peddocks's East Head. Modeled after family eco-retreats in the Virgin Islands, the all-inclusive camp would build low-tech camping facilities, such

A homemade sign in a crumbling home on Peddocks Island aims to make a political point. When owners die, the cottages are taken over by the Commonwealth's Department of Conservation and Recreation.

as three-season tent cabins, and provide education programs, kayaking, swimming, fishing and stargazing for parents and children who want to stay overnight on the island. Buildings on Fort Andrews, including the former firehouse and bakery, would be rehabilitated and used for community purposes, such as a communal dining facility. A former administration building, located near what was once the fort's parade grounds, would be turned into an open-air amphitheatre. The renovated chapel would be used for meetings, weddings or other events. Showers, hot food and other services would be offered. The plan also proposes rehabbing one of the fort's buildings into a conference center, a facility that—being so close to Boston—could bring much-needed income to the national park. Of all the Harbor Islands, Peddocks is the best choice for such development.

Preparation for the family eco-camp has begun. The Islands Partnership has invested about $5 million installing utility and waterlines from Hull to Peddocks, making it possible to provide running water and electricity on the island once again. The next step will be to determine which of the remaining Fort Andrews buildings can be saved. The price of renovation is huge: it will cost an estimated $415,000 to demolish one unsafe building, at least $5 million to stabilize and rehab other structures and $1.5 million to fix the chapel. In the meantime, the island is closed to camping and the fort is off-limits.

What of the cottages? Some have suggested turning them into a summer artists' colony or creating an association in which members would pay to be entered into a lottery to win a summer stay on Peddocks; both models have been used successfully in other areas of the country. Such proposals, however, raise questions of how to maintain the houses and bring them up to required safety codes.

There are no easy answers for Peddocks. Yet the living history here is worth preserving, even if it presents huge challenges that will require compromise, creativity and a boatload of money.

Months after my conversation with a Peddocks ranger on the island's cinematic appeal, I learned that filmmakers for a Martin Scorsese production of Dennis Lehane's *Shutter Island* (retitled *Ashcliffe* for the screen) had spent time filming on Peddocks. So Peddocks may win screen time as a "stand-in" for the mythical Shutter Island. The future of the real Peddocks remains, however, a cliffhanger. We'll have to wait to see what happens to the cottage dwellers and Fort Andrews before the finale is written and the credits roll.

CHAPTER 9

the creature from gallops, and the other lost islands

Day comes with a cool rush on Lovells Island. I crawl like an arthritic snake out of my sleeping bag and get the stove going. A cup of coffee in hand, I stumble to the shore, hoping daylight will jumpstart my joints. As I sip the java and feel the sun jog my sluggish blood, I stare longingly at a verdant island so close I can almost smell the damp from its trees. From my perch on the shore of Lovells, I can see a pier and what looks like a gazebo in a mass of green. Just as Lovells once tempted me with her long, low sandbars and salt marsh, now this island calls to me with its lush tangle of green.

It's a call I can't answer. All around the island are placards (in neon that says "We mean business") warning everyone to stay away. Forbidden. Stay out. That means you. And your little dog, too.

The 16.4-acre Gallops Island is closed to visitors. Officially closed, that is, since 2000. It sits there, a green gem just minutes (by boat) from Lovells and Georges, and no one can go there. Why is it forbidden, an island non grata? What terrible things lurk in that lush forest? What is the creature from Gallops that haunts the nightmares of the park rangers? And is the fair island of Gallops lost to us forever?

When I made my first trip to the Boston Harbor Islands, the maps of the park service still showed the ferry lines stopping at Gallops. I have since run into dozens of people who have spent time on the island who described it to me in glowing terms. Not a few have called it their "favorite island." Kathy Abbott, the founding executive director of the Island Alliance who is now with the Trustees of Reservations, gushed over a "secret beach" there. And Ellen Berkland, an archaeologist for the City of Boston, called it, "Magical. Small. Walkable. Lots to see."

For now we will see nothing. And the reason why lies in the multiple uses of the island.

Gallops Island, an island known for its unusual plant life and history as an army radio school, is closed to the public due to concerns about asbestos contamination. *Courtesy of* Boston Herald.

Before the Europeans came, Native Americans used Gallops, along with other islands, as a summer residence. During the early colonial period, the island was owned by Captain John Gallops; until his death around 1650, he used it for grazing cattle and growing grain. The island bore his name, although in the hit-or-miss spelling of island history it has also been called "Gallup's Island." Like many colonists, John Gallops had an issue with trees—the fewer of them the better—and between him and other colonists, Gallops was stripped of most of its oak and aspen, and the land was used for farming for decades. In the early nineteenth century, Gallops (often called Newcomb's Island, after one of its subsequent owners) "was occupied by the well-known 'Joe Snow' and became a famous resort for pleasure parties, and his name will long be remembered by the numerous persons who have partaken of his good cheer and remarkable style of his hospitality," Stark wrote in his 1879 book on Boston Harbor.

During the Civil War, a training camp was built on Gallops, with as many as three thousand recruits staying there. Regiments returning from the war were quartered there, including the Fifty-fourth Regiment of black soldiers, the outfit celebrated in the 1989 movie *Glory*. In 1866, a quarantine hospital was opened on Gallops to accommodate immigrants and other travelers who often arrived on these shores with diseases such as smallpox and cholera. Soon a medical staff was examining more than thirty-three thousand people a year. Some locals ended up at this hospital as well, including victims of a smallpox epidemic that struck Boston in 1879. Indeed, into the early 1900s, newspapers carried stories of unfortunates—such as immigrants with leprosy—who would be detained at the island, treated in the hospital or—in the case of lepers—transferred to a leper colony, never to walk among the general public again. The hospital continued to operate on the island until around 1937.

Gallops was also a part of the country's coastal defenses, the network of forts and fortifications that reached from Fort Winthrop on Governors Island, Fort Warren on Georges Island, Fort Strong on Long Island and Fort Andrews on Peddocks Island. On Gallops, the U.S. government operated a school for training radio operators. Between 1940 and 1969, more than five thousand men attended the radio school housed in a large, two-story facility. Photos of the time show Gallops teeming with military officials, barracks and other buildings. After World War II, the radio school was closed and the buildings were dismantled and demolished. All that remains of the radio school today is its foundation.

Perhaps one of the more striking features of Gallops is its unusual plant life. Dr. Alvin Sweeney, the director at the quarantine hospital, was a gifted amateur horticulturalist who grew exotic species such as the bladder senna from the Himalayas. He or others also introduced such nonnative plants as lilac, forsythia and rambler roses. Sweeney planted ornamental trees and shrubs, including peach, pear and apple trees. Even after the hospital closed, Sweeney's plants and trees continued to thrive. Island volunteers have told me about the good times when they brought out presses, picked apples and pressed their own cider. In 1973, Gallops was acquired by the Commonwealth of Massachusetts, becoming one of the sixteen islands in the Boston Harbor State Park. For years, water shuttles took visitors there on a daily basis in the summer.

Looking at a self-guided tour brochure of that era, now a sort of collector's item, I can see that trails crisscrossed the island to various lookouts for views of Peddocks, Rainsford and Long Island, leading past the foundations of a stable that had been used over the years. There were picnic tables and outhouses. The brochure noted holes left in a tree by a yellow-bellied sapsucker and warned visitors off a bluff used as a nesting area by gulls in spring and early summer.

But in the late 1990s, park officials discovered asbestos-containing tiles, called transite, on the island. The military had used these tiles in the building of its facilities. When the buildings were demolished, the debris was buried.

A view of the crumbling Fort Winthrop on Governors Island in 1940. The island is now part of Logan Airport. *Courtesy of* Boston Herald.

Unfortunately, over the years, the land eroded and the tiles were exposed. The fibers of asbestos; cause tumors in the lungs and other serious diseases if inhaled. Park officials have attempted to clean up the asbestos; about nine tons of asbestos have been removed from the island, but at least another $8 million would be necessary for more study and work to finish the cleanup. When efforts to keep the public away from contaminated areas on the island were deemed unsuccessful, the entire island was closed. Park officials have sought money from the military for cleanup—you broke it, you fix it, being, I gather, the legal argument. The response from the military (and this is my interpretation of what officials don't actually say) has been, "Take a number and wait in line."

Asbestos is generally more dangerous after continued or prolonged exposure, and various volunteers have wondered if the stuff on Gallops is an immediate threat to the infrequent visitor. But no one wants to take the risk. If children are on the island, playing as children do, there is a chance one may ingest or inhale some of this material. Given the situation, park officials believe they have no choice but to declare Gallops off-limits. In our hyper-alert—some would say litigious—society, there are few other options. For the immediate future, Gallops is a lost island.

Indeed, Boston Harbor is filled with lost islands. Here are a few notable ones:

GOVERNORS ISLAND: Located off the shore of East Boston, this was a favorite island of historian Edward Rowe Snow, who declared in 1945 that "as far as casual visitors are concerned, it is safe to say (Governors Island) was the best-known island in all of New England." First called Conant's Island after its first white owner, it was later leased to John Winthrop, the first governor of the Commonwealth, in return for a hogshead of the best wine produced there—and later, when the quality of the drink seemed dubious, for two bushels of apples. The island went through a variety of owners, although it was used primarily for agriculture until 1808, when a fort was built there named for Joseph Warren, a hero of the Revolutionary War. The name of Fort Warren later went to the fortifications being built on Georges Island, and Fort Winthrop was later established in 1846 on Governors. Only a small regiment was ever based there.

Fort Winthrop was a pleasant place for a seaside outing, unless you count the day of September 8, 1902. On that otherwise balmy Sunday, Governors Island was rocked by a huge explosion. An estimated ten to twelve thousand pounds of powder stored in a magazine at Fort Winthrop blew up, sending rocks and debris flying among nearby pleasure seekers and up to a quarter mile offshore. At least one man was killed and several went missing; only parts of their bodies were found. The force of the explosion rattled china on the mainland. The redoubt in which the magazine was located was "entirely obliterated," according to a *Boston Globe* account. Newspapers speculated that sparks from one of the victims' pipes sparked the blaze, but army engineering personnel said the explosion would probably remain a mystery. "There will be no use in excavating in the ruins," Captain Harry Taylor told the *Globe*. "If there was anyone in the magazine, then he would be blown to atoms…In my opinion the man who caused the explosion blew up with the magazine."

After the First World War, the U.S. military took over the island, but Boston Mayor James M. Curley included it in the plans for an expanded airport. A March 29, 1936 story in the *Boston Herald* declared that the island was leased from the federal government for fifty years for one dollar and would be used to give Boston "the best airport and dirigible landing base in the world." That unfortunate Hindenburg incident in 1937 put a damper on the desire for air blimp travel, but Governors Island was flattened out, beginning in 1946, and became part of the airport.

APPLE ISLAND: This was once a small green island, north of Governors, noted as a beautiful spot used for farming and later for revels and picnicking. It apparently had a lone apple tree that was used as a marker for vessels coming into the harbor. According to an August 25, 1901 article in the *Boston Globe*, "It has been twice the property of the city, once owned by an Englishman and once by a man living in Ireland. It has been a contagious disease station, a summer home, a cow pasture, a prize ring and lastly, a picnic-ground for the political organizations that have taken their outings in the harbor." The article also recounts a ghost story, later repeated by Snow, about the days when Apple Island was the home of robbers and thieves and a beautiful young girl was found murdered off its shores. From the *Globe*:

> *The community was horrified, and her sweetheart was said to have gone to the island and joined the band of thieves just to discover who had killed his lady love. After some weeks, his corpse was found hanging from the largest tree that is still standing on the island, and the robbers were not heard of again. The ghosts of the two unfortunate young people were said to walk up and down the sands and underneath the trees, moaning and weeping, and in recent years, this old ghost story has cropped up again and again.*

Perhaps the pair now wanders the lost baggage area. Apple Island, along with Governors and the small Bird Island, was incorporated into Logan Airport in 1946.

NODDLES ISLAND: Noddles, once located off the shore of what is now East Boston and named for owner William Noddle, was the site of shipbuilding by Donald McKay, known for his fast clipper ships. (A monument to McKay stands on Castle Island.) A month before the famous Battle for Bunker Hill in June of 1775, Noddles Island was the scene of a skirmish between revolutionaries and the British, primarily over livestock that the Patriots wanted to keep out of the bellies of the British. The Battle of Noddles Island set the stage for the better-known Bunker Hill fight that followed. Noddles, which according to *Islands of Boston Harbor* had seventy thousand residents in 1932, became part of the mainland when landfill was gradually used to extend the borders of Boston. This was also the fate of Hog Island, also called Susanna Island. According to Edward Snow, Hog Island was owned in 1687 by the famous New England Judge Samuel Sewall, who presided over the Salem witch trials and later came to regret his decisions there. Hog/Susanna Island is now part of the Orient Heights neighborhood of East Boston.

LITTLE HOG ISLAND: Some may argue that this small island, off the coast of Hull in Hingham Bay, has not been lost at all but just reborn as Spinnaker Island. It was once praised by Henry David Thoreau, who was quoted in *Islands of Boston Harbor Illustrated* as writing: "As I looked over the water, I saw the islands rapidly wasting away, the sea nibbling voraciously at the

An aerial shot of Governors Island in 1936, before it became part of Logan Airport. *Courtesy of* Boston Herald.

Continent. On the other hand, these wrecks of isles were being fancifully arranged into new shores, as at Hog Island, inside of Hull, where everything seemed to be gently lapsing into futurity." Used by colonists for agriculture, Little Hog Island was taken over by the military in the 1920s for the building of Fort Duvall, with its concrete batteries and sixteen-inch guns. During the Cold War, Little Hog housed an Integrated Fire Control and radar system for a Nike missile site located in what is now Webb Memorial State Park. The missile site was deactivated in the 1970s.

In the late 1980s, the island was taken over by a developer who built a causeway to the island, constructed condominiums and gave the spot the sailing-chic name of Spinnaker Island. It is not part of the national park. A guard shack at the entrance of the causeway wards off the casual visitor. In *The Boston Harbor Islands: A History of an Urban Wilderness*, David Kales comments that "Thoreau would roll over in his grave if he saw the abomination of the once-bucolic Hog Island transmogrified into the rabbit warren condominiums of today's Spinnaker Island."

Perhaps it's not really fair to say Little Hog Island has been "lost." But it is fair to point out that, had the state and other advocates not pushed to protect them, many of the Harbor Islands might have been Spinnakerized, that is, turned into private sea-view hideaways, off limits to anybody but owners and their guests.

Is Gallops Island really lost? Park officials continue to cite its cleanup as a top concern. Others tell me that what Gallops needs is its own advocacy group, its own constituency, a LSG (Let's Save Gallops) organization that would pressure the appropriate politicians to fund the cleanup. But many people just don't know about Gallops, and those who do—I sometimes suspect—may be content with their memories or the occasional trip. A few risk-taking souls simply ignore the orange signs, and hike or camp illegally on the island.

Would the island need a total makeover like that of Spectacle? Capping Gallops would surely destroy all the quirks that make it charming. Would we have to destroy the island in order to save it? Perhaps not. Asbestos cleanup is not a new science; it has been done before. "Environmental cleanup happens all the time," Susan Kane, DCR district manager, remarked to me. Then why not Gallops? Simply, "It's not in anyone's backyard."

Park officials have repeatedly said a cleanup of Gallops is one of their priorities. Until that day comes, the creatures that live on Gallops have the island—more or less—to themselves.

CHAPTER 10

tragedy on thompson island

S tanding on Thompson Island, the angle of the world seems off-kilter.
From where I'm standing I can see the rainbow shades of Sister
Corita Kent's famous splash-paint decoration on the gas tank that sits
along Interstate 93 on Boston's southern shore. I'm very used to staring
at this famous landmark, painted in 1971 by the nun turned artist who
also created the Love Stamp for the U.S. Postal Service. But usually when
I'm contemplating the gas tank, I'm also fuming with hundreds of other
motorists stuck in the city's hellish traffic on I-93, as we inch our way
through Boston's Dorchester neighborhood.

But although the familiar gas tank is in plain sight, I feel like I'm viewing
it from another state—certainly from another state of mind. I'm standing
with a group of visitors at the edge of a green, lush, watery carpet, a forty-
acre salt marsh that stretches to the ocean. One person in the tour group
is bravely attempting to cross a rope bridge, something that our guide has
called the "monkey bridge," his feet only inches away from slick mud.
Others in the group have binoculars pressed to their eyes, but even without
that assistance I can pick up the white bird, a snowy egret, that perches in
the green trees at the edge of the marsh. A great blue heron suddenly comes
into view, sailing majestically above the tall grasses of the marsh.

With about 170 upland acres, Thompson Island is one of the larger
Harbor Islands and one of the most diverse. In a two-hour tour led by a
park ranger, my group has walked through the campus of the Outward
Bound Education Center (which owns the island), roamed over rolling
meadows, visited an old cemetery, watched a shorebird suck down a worm,
peered at a green crab that nearly blended into its watery surroundings
and walked along a rocky beach speculating on the source of the bits of
dull red bricks that dot the shoreline. We passed a sixty-foot climbing tower

A visitor ventures across a rope bridge on Thompson Island. The rainbow colors of the gas tank painted by Sister Corita Kent in the 1970s can be seen in the distance.

designed to hone the athletic skills of young people and also to teach them trust, since climbers often have to rely on others for safety. As we walked past, craning our necks to stare at this incongruous configuration of log and rope, someone in the group quipped, "Last one up is *smart*."

A visit to Thompson provides a different kind of look at the Boston Harbor Islands. During the summer, the privately owned island is usually open once a week to the general public. The Thompson Outward Bound Education Center is a nonprofit organization aimed at providing adventurous and challenging experiences for adolescents from all economic and social communities. The center runs and maintains a number of buildings on the island, including a conference center, an administrative building, a gym and playing fields. Its programs are part of a long tradition on the islands of helping young people.

In the seventeenth century, Thompson was one of the first islands to have a full-time European resident. In 1619, a Scotsman named David Thompson built a trading post on the southeast side of the island and traded with the native people who lived in the area. The thirty-foot-square brick trading post was abandoned after Thompson died in 1628, and there is speculation that some of the worn bricks scattered on the shore might be from Thompson's original building. The island was acquired by the community of Dorchester in 1634 and was used for farming.

Starting in 1833, the island housed an institution aimed at helping young boys into adulthood. The Boston Asylum for Indigent Boys, formed in 1814 to aid boys left destitute by the War of 1812, moved its facilities to Thompson in 1833; in 1835, it merged with the Boston Farm School and thereafter was often referred to as the Farm School. Enrolling boys ages seven to twelve, the school was also a working farm that taught boys carpentry, printing, blacksmithing, shoe repair and other skills. For many young men, the island was their home until they reached twenty-one, at which time they returned to their families or went into trade. The school formed a band in 1857, often claimed to be the first school band in the country. As New England industrialized, the school began to emphasize trades over farming and, in 1907, changed its name to the Farm and Trade School. In the mid-1950s, the school was renamed Thompson Academy and in 1975 it became the Thompson Island Educational Center. The school became part of Outward Bound in the mid-1980s and now offers programs for both girls and boys, as well as adult leadership programs.

While the school's main building burned down in 1971, many of the red brick buildings from the original campus remain, although they are generally off-limits to the casual visitor. With either a self-guided tour brochure or a Park Service guide, visitors are allowed to explore the island's beaches, meadows, fields and woodlands.

Landmarks on the island include the stone foundation of a root cellar, built to house vegetables for the school during the long winter months, and the remains of a weather station where boys once recorded temperature, humidity, dew point, rainfall, wind speed and other meteorological information three times a day. The site has a curious "boot scrape," perhaps to aid the boys when wet weather turned the ground to mud.

Not only does the island include a forty-acre salt marsh that shelters many birds, but in 2007 a former salt marsh on the island's eastern shore was restored. United States Geological Survey topographic maps from 1903 and 1946 show the area to have once been a salt marsh, but debris and rubble

A visitor checks the interior of a root cellar, built with stones, which once kept produce cool on Thompson Island.

later clogged an outlet, preventing tidal flow and creating a brackish pond that promoted the growth of the invasive phragmites. In 2007 the channel was unblocked, with the aim of bringing back the tidal flow and recreating the tidal pool.

Balancing Thompson's natural beauty is, however, the story of its "lost boys." At the southern tip of the island is a small burial site marked by two signs. One is a weather-beaten wooden plaque, with these words scratched in makeshift fashion: "Two tragedies of the Boston Harbor, in 1842 and 1892, drowned these boys. May the water and winds bless their souls, may their souls bless our hearts and our island." Below those words are faint marks that could be names, indecipherable now in the gray wood. The second sign, less weatherworn and more official looking, explains that in April 1842 twenty-three students from the island died during a boating excursion given as a reward for good conduct, and that in April 1892 the lives of eight boys were lost when the school's sloop capsized in a sudden squall.

There were no such signs on this spot when Carol Fithian, a volunteer with the Friends of the Boston Harbor Islands, made her first trip to Thompson in the early 1990s. At that time only a few bricks marked the area where the boys had been buried; the plot also contained the remains

TWO TRAGEDIES OF THE BOSTON HARBOR,
IN 1842 AND 1892, DROWNED THESE BOYS.

MAY THE WATER AND WINDS BLESS THEIR
SOULS; MAY THEIR SOULS BLESS OUR
HEARTS AND OUR ISLAND.

GEORGE CHASE	WILLIAM CLARKE	ISAAC MAJOR
JAMES TRACEY	HENRY McCLEAN	ABRAHAM SPENCE
PATRICK SHEAN	ROBERT WALKER	HENRY BURNHAM
SAMUEL WALKER	JAMES CHANDLER	MICHAEL WHITE
R.G. WHITE	JOHN JOHNSON	ROBERT WALKER
CHARLES AUSTIN	THOMAS DOLAND	JOSHUA OAKS
JOHN HALL	THOMAS BLAKE	MR. THOMAS
HENRY LUCAS	JAMES WALKER	PEABODY
JAMES FILLMORE	PETER PASTROUCHE	

In 2002 a sixth-grade class of the Willauer School, an independent school then operating on Thompson, built a sign to commemorate the boating accident that took the lives of twenty-three boys, an instructor and a boat keeper in April of 1842. *Photo by Christine Jones, National Park Service ranger.*

of Native Americans who had been found on the island. A guide talked of the accidents but only in general terms. Afterward, Fithian could not get the tragedy out of her mind. Who were these boys? What were their names? Shouldn't they be remembered in some way? "I thought it was important that someone know who these children were," she told me. So Fithian set off to do some research.

She found that in April of 1842, twenty-three boys ranging in age from eight to sixteen—almost half the Thompson school's total enrollment—were given a reward for good behavior: a fishing trip. On their way back to the island, as fellow students on shore were cheering the students on, the boat tipped over and filled with water; it quickly sank. A nearby schooner tried to pick up the boys, but all but four of the boys drowned. The boat keeper and a schoolmaster were also lost. "It is one of those events of an inscrutable

Providence, which occurring suddenly to so many youthful spirits, in the moment of joyous exhilaration, and sending sorrow and mourning into so many families, cannot but excite in the breast of everyone a sympathy for the bereaved families, and a living sense of the frail tenure of human existence," wrote the *Boston Daily Advertiser* on April 30, 1842.

Fifty years later, another tragedy struck. On the night of April 10, 1892, about ten boys rowed from the school to City Point to bring instructor Anders Frederick Nordberg back to the school. They picked up the teacher and set sail for the return journey. The wind was gentle, the moon was bright and the young captain Frank Hitchcock was at the tiller, according to a *Boston Globe* story dated April 12, 1892. Suddenly a blast of wind caught the sail and overturned the boat. The instructor, Nordberg, went under and did not surface. The boys held onto the overturned rig until, one by one, they succumbed to the cold and sank into the water. Young George Ellis was the second to go and "in the moonlight we could see (his face) plainly, and it bore such a sad expression, as it disappeared from sight, that the memory of it will always be with me," sixteen-year-old Walter Clemmenson later told the *Globe*. One of the other boys in the water started crying out, "I see a light," but the others told him that that was impossible. The boy kept repeating the words until he was exhausted. "Boys, the light has gone out," he whispered, before he too sunk into the black water.

Finally only Clemmenson and Charles Lind were left clinging to the boat. After several hours, the boat drifted into shallow waters near Spectacle, and Clemmenson was able to wade ashore and get help. The two boys recovered, later learning that a night watchman had waved a lantern on the shores of Thompson earlier in the night, apparently the light that one of the lost boys had seen.

In 2002, Fithian helped a sixth-grade class of the Willauer School, an independent school then operating on Thompson, with the restoration of the cemetery by providing them with a list of the names of the drowned boys. These sixth graders built the sign that stands at the burial plot and included the names of the deceased boys. They also held a ceremony, at which they read letters they had written to their long lost fellow students. It was the first recognition in modern times of the victims buried there, Fithian said. More recently, Fithian has been contacted by the great-grandson of Walter Clemmenson, a West Virginia man who plans to visit the island where his ancestor so narrowly escaped death.

Today, the wooden sign made by the sixth graders is weathered and the names are faded. Fithian hopes that someday a more permanent marker will be installed to keep alive the memories of children who met their deaths in the springtime just off the shores of Thompson Island.

CHAPTER 11

seeing the light: boston's oldest lighthouse station

Maybe Little Brewster Island isn't really at the end of the world, but you can definitely see it from here. As the boat nears this small island, I'm gazing east beyond the lighthouse, and all I can see is the unbroken line of the Atlantic; the next stop, it seems, is Europe. When I turn west, I can see the city skyline shimmering eight miles away. It feels like eighty. The sea rocks the boat as we attempt a tricky landing at the swaying dock, where a woman in a long skirt and bonnet braces herself against the wind and waves a kerchief. This is Sally R. Snowman, the seventieth (by her count) keeper of Boston Light, the distinctive lighthouse that has sat on Little Brewster since the late 1700s.

When tours come in, Snowman likes to dress the part. Dr. Snowman (she has a PhD in education) displays a passion for her work that rivals the ardor of other Harbor Islands advocates. Snowman first visited Little Brewster at age ten with her father, a member of the Coast Guard auxiliary, and has been in love with the place ever since. Now, not only is she the first female Boston Light lighthouse keeper, and not only did she write a definitive history of the lighthouse in 1999, but also she and husband James G. Thomson were married here in 1994. The pair lives most of the year on what is essentially a large rock jutting out of the Atlantic. They help maintain the oldest continuously operating lighthouse station and the second oldest lighthouse structure in the United States. (Boston Light would probably be the oldest lighthouse in the United States but for those sore losers, the British, who torched the original lighthouse on their way out of town in 1776.) Day and night, every day of the year, Boston Light sends its beacon over the ocean, rays that can be seen—on a clear day—for twenty-seven miles. No matter how blasé you might be about maritime history or equipment, you have to admit that lighthouses are still pretty cool.

Sally Snowman is the seventieth (by her count) keeper of Boston Light and the first female keeper of the oldest lighthouse station in the United States.

Images of Boston Light virtually define the Boston Harbor Islands National Park. The lighthouse is the central image in the park's logo, and photographs of the white-walled tower on its rocky perch dominate the covers of most books on the Boston Harbor Islands, this book being a rare exception. (Seriously, it's hard to take a bad photograph of Boston Light.) At about three acres, depending on the tide, the island of Little Brewster barely rises above the water. For such a small place, it packs a huge history.

In the early eighteenth century, city officials saw a need for lighthouses to guide the increasing number of ships passing in and out of Boston Harbor. In June 1715, a court order was passed calling for the erection of a lighthouse to be built and maintained from funds collected as duties on ships entering the harbor. In 1716, a sixty-foot tower was built of granite rubblestone on Little Brewster, selected for its strategic position off Hull and near the "intersection" of the channels of Nantasket Roads and Black Rock Channel. A keeper's house, barn and wharf were also constructed. At that time, light was produced by wicks immersed in fish or whale oil burned behind a glass lens—not exactly the safest or most pleasant method, due to excessive smoke and hot dripping oil, according to *Boston Light: A Historical Perspective*, the authoritative book on the lighthouse written by Snowman and her husband, James Thomson. In June of 1716, forty-three-year-old George Worthylake was appointed the first keeper, and the beacon was lit by September. Worthylake lasted only two years. Worthylake, his wife Anne, his daughter Ruth, his slave Shadwell and a family friend named John Edge were all lost when their boat capsized as they were returning from an outing. The next keeper, Robert Saunders, also drowned, this time just two days into the job; it was lucky, Snowman dryly observed in an interview with me, that the harbor was able to get a third keeper.

Despite the fate of the first two keepers, the beacon stayed lit, more or less, until 1775, when the site became a strategic target for American revolutionaries seeking to disrupt British rule in the colonies. The insurgents managed to damage the light. When the British finally left Boston in June 1776, Redcoat soldiers landed on the island and blew up what was left of the lighthouse, although some of the bricks may have been salvaged and used for rebuilding the structure. In 1783, the Commonwealth of Massachusetts decided that the beacon should return, and by December 1783, the lighthouse was rebuilt and the sixth keeper began his duties. By 1790, Boston Light and other lighthouses were ceded to the U.S. federal government, which was now assuming control over the expanding national waterways. In 1939, the lighthouse came under the jurisdiction of the newly formed U.S. Coast Guard, created by the merger of several lifesaving organizations and the lighthouse service.

The view from inside the tower of Boston Light. *Photo by Don Cann, National Park Service ranger, courtesy of Boston Harbor Islands Alliance.*

The general silhouette of the tower and the island has changed little in 225 years. Five bands of steel were placed around the tower in 1809 to prevent it from bulging, an addition that distinguishes it from other New England lighthouses. In 1859, the tower was raised to its current height (just about one hundred feet) to accommodate a new lens. In 1974, aluminum bands replaced the rusting steel bands.

Technology has changed the way its beacon is produced, replacing burning oil with electricity. In 1859, a 1,000-watt lamp was placed in a new 9-foot Fresnel lens; the lens's 336 individual prisms and 12 so-called "bull's eyes" magnify the light to two million candlepower. Though the light appears to be blinking on and off, Snowman explains that it is not actually flashing; rather, the lens is rotating and creating spokes of light—the same beams that can be seen sweeping over the town of Hull. Except for a period during World War II when it was feared that the light would guide enemy warplanes, the light has remained on.

About sixty-nine keepers have come and gone from this tiny island. Some gave their life in their duties, and many of them raised families and grew old on this postage stamp in the ocean. Up until the early twentieth century, the keepers had no running water (water was collected in a cistern that was also used to

A trip to the Harbor Islands may get you acquainted with seabirds.

produce steam for the fog signal) and no indoor plumbing. Over the years, the keeper's house has been modernized. The current house, built in 1884 in what has been called stick-style Victorian, now has a full bath, a microwave oven and other staples of modern life. Snowman still doesn't get mail delivery, but she has a mobile phone. Boston Light has withstood the fierce storms that batter the New England coast, including the Hurricane of 1938, the infamous Blizzard of 1978, which destroyed the island's steel pier, and the so-called "Perfect Storm" of 1991. In 1986, Little Brewster Island was included in the National Registry of Historic Places. In 1991, the lighthouse was opened to the public for tours.

By the 1990s, the U.S. Coast Guard had automated all other United States lighthouses and was planning to do the same for Boston Light in 1998. But, after appeals by preservation groups, a law was passed mandating that while the light would be automated, the island would continue to be staffed with U.S Coast Guard personnel. After September 11, 2001, however, the Coast Guard decided Boston Light personnel were needed for other port security duties; the law was changed to allow Coast Guard auxiliary members to serve as lighthouse keepers. In 2003 Snowman, an auxiliary member, longtime volunteer on Little Brewster and lighthouse historian, applied for and won the dream job of her life. While she doesn't actually turn the light on and off, she is one of those responsible for maintaining the light, watching over the grounds and telling people the story of Boston Light.

When I first met Snowman and her husband in the summer of 2007, their enthusiasm for their work seemed not a whit dimmed. She delights in dressing in period outfits, and her husband relishes wearing a "Keeper's Husband" T-shirt while the pair show visitors around the island. They are generally at the lighthouse Wednesday through Sunday

Edward Rowe Snow, his wife and daughter carried on the tradition of the "Flying Santas" by delivering holiday packages to lighthouse keepers and their families along the New England coast. *Courtesy of* Boston Herald.

during the summer and come out twice a month in the winter. Life on the edge seems to suit Snowman. She speaks of watching orange-pink sunsets and of seeing all kinds of seabirds and waterfowl, even a snowy owl that would visit from Great Brewster. In September, clouds of monarch butterflies flutter by Little Brewster, part of their migration south. "This place speaks to me," she says, her words echoing those of other Boston Harbor Islands visitors.

A visit to Boston Light can be a bracing journey. I caught the National Park Service–led tour to Little Brewster on a day of rough seas but clear skies. Less than an hour after leaving Boston, I was walking from the pier onto the granite ledge, 800 feet long and 250 feet wide, that forms the island. The first stop was the boathouse, now used as a visitors' center, where Snowman or other Coast Guard auxiliary personnel greet visitors with a quick talk and question and answer session. The boathouse has numerous historic photographs, including shots of lighthouse keepers waving to "Flying Santas," small-craft pilots who traditionally brought Christmas packages and other treats to lighthouse keepers and their families along the coast. (Bill Wincapaw started the tradition in 1927, and Edward Rowe Snow maintained the practice from 1936 to 1979.) Lighthouse keepers also had a tradition of keeping dogs and cats as companions, and in the boathouse there's a photo of a raccoon that found its way onto the island in 1916 and became the pet of the keeper's wife. The current island mascots seem to be a pair of wild muskrats dubbed Jimmy and Jane. Another popular lighthouse mascot in the 1990s was a black lab named Sammy. Snowman once told a *Globe* correspondent that Sammy used to bark every night about dusk; Snowman calls that time of day the "Shadwell Hour," in honor of the slave who died with the first lighthouse keeper. The ill-fated Shadwell is also credited with a lot of spooky events on Little Brewster. In his lighthouse book, D'Entremont recounts a tale from the 1940s in which the lighthouse keeper's wife claimed she heard a little girl's sobbing voice calling "Shaaaaadwell." Moreover, the woman insists she did not learn until later that the drowned slave was named Shadwell.

From the boathouse, paths lead to the keeper's house, an oil house and the island's cistern and the tower itself. A red-tipped object that looks like a missile is actually a "red nun buoy," or floating navigation aid. Used with green cans, the red pointy "nuns" marked safe passages. More artifacts are on display in a small museum at the base of the lighthouse tower, including examples of the prisms used for the beacon and the so-called "great gun" or cannon once used as a signaling device in the fog. Thought to date to the late seventeenth or mid-eighteenth century, the cannon was retired in 1851

Graves Light today.

A postcard circa 1909 of Graves Light. *Courtesy of Kathy Alpert.*

and replaced by a bell. In 1993 it was returned to the island from a Coast Guard museum. Today, an electronic signal, which goes on automatically when sensors pick up moisture in the area, provides warnings during a fog.

The lighthouse tower is scheduled to be open for visitation in the summer of 2008; the tower was closed to visitation in 2007 due to legal issues regarding warranty of the restored antique Fresnel lens. Because of the delicacy of the mechanism, the tower can only be visited on an official tour. Little Brewster, Snowman likes to point out, is a working site, owned and operated by the U.S. Coast Guard. "To climb the tower is a privilege, not a right," she says.

Some tours to Boston Light extend the journey with a jaunt to Graves Light, a 113-foot lighthouse built about 1905 on "the Graves," a mass of rocks named for Admiral Thomas Graves. From its perch northeast of the Brewsters, this granite lighthouse seems even more remote than Boston Light (the name is far more ominous, let's face it) and was automated in the 1970s. The Graves is a favorite site for bird-watching, particularly in the winter, when waterfowl come south. Purple sandpipers, double-crested and great cormorants are often glimpsed on the rocks, while loons, surf scooters, brant geese, common eider, buffleheads, red-breasted mergansers and various kinds of gulls can be seen in the waters nearby.

Another distinctive New England lighthouse—and the subject of many postcards in the early nineteenth century—is Minot's Light, built in 1860 on Cohasset Rocks, off the South Shore towns of Cohasset and Scituate. This lighthouse, which has a long history, is outside the boundaries of the national park.

Even today, when we have radar, GPS devices and Google maps to help us find our way on the high seas or to a friend's home in the next town over, there's something romantic about a lighthouse. It's the beacon that lights up the dark, the proverbial light in the storm. Images of Boston Light may be a beacon to retail—you see the image popping up on T-shirts, books and postcards—but little compares to seeing the Light in person. Bring a camera.

CHAPTER 12

meet the brewsters

At the edge of the map of the Boston Harbor Islands, you'll see a cluster of little specks denoting Shag Rocks, Green Island, Little Calf Island, Calf Island, Outer Brewster Island, Middle Brewster Island, Great Brewster Island and Little Brewster Island. Collectively, they are commonly referred to as the Brewsters (although not all are Brewsters per se). Close to the town of Hull, which owned some of them at one time, these islands were used by the military for fortifications, particularly Battery Jewel on Outer Brewster Island. The Brewsters were the homes of poor fishermen, hermits and some of Boston's wealthiest men and women. Let's meet a few of the Brewsters.

"Ye Square Partie" on Great Brewster

From the shores of Little Brewster, Great Brewster looms like a big older brother, its drumlin peak rising from a sea-walled shore. At about twenty acres, Great Brewster is the largest of the outer islands in the harbor. Great Brewster offers a landscape of two hills, a marsh, a beach and sea walls that attempt to keep erosion at bay. The bluffs provide great views of the harbor, including the sight of both Boston Light and Graves Light. Like the other islands, Great Brewster has a history of farming and fortification. It was named for Elder William Brewster, a leader in the Plymouth Colony. Around the turn of the century, it was the site of the summer cottages of many Bostonians, as well as fishermen. It was also used by the U.S. military for coastal defense. Today, one can still see remains of a bunker and an observation post.

Depending on the tide, you may be able to see Great Brewster Spit, a slice of land that reaches more than a mile toward Georges and Lovells Islands.

Bug Light, a navigational aide near Great Brewster Island, got its name because people thought it resembled an insect. It was a popular subject for postcards in the early 1900s. *Courtesy of Kathy Alpert.*

A sand spit often connects Great and Little Brewster Islands, which in the past allowed the lighthouse keeper on Little Brewster to visit with families summering on the larger island. Just offshore are pilings of the Narrows Light Station. Built in 1856, Bug Light, so called because of its resemblance to a spindly legged insect, was a marker for passing ships. A very popular subject for postcards in the early twentieth century, Bug Light was destroyed by fire in 1929 and replaced by an automated beacon in 1930. The east side of the island serves as a breeding ground and nursery for herring and great black backed gulls, which hatch in June. Both Great Brewster and Middle Brewster once were getaway spots for wealthy Bostonians, who built houses of their own there or rented houses for a week at a time.

I was able to take a trip to Great Brewster one cold winter's day in early 2008 without ever having to leave the Boston shore. I spent the afternoon with four intrepid women of the nineteenth century, courtesy of the Schlesinger Library of the Radcliffe Institute for Advanced Study at Harvard. The library's collection contains a diary, well-worn as if often read over the years, written by a woman who spent two weeks on Great Brewster in 1891 with three close friends.

The women, who identified themselves only by their nicknames—the Autocrat, the Aristocrat, the Acrobat and the Scribe—stayed from July 15 to July 31 in a rustic cottage on what they called "an enchanted island." For them, it was a time of exquisite freedom. The diary kept by the Scribe, who was actually Helen Augusta Whittier (1846–1925), called their adventure "Ye Square Partie at Ye Great Brewster." Whittier described the foursome's daily activities—the books they read, the meals they prepared (cold tongue, tomatoes, salt pork, quince pie) and the games they played. The diary even has small, faded photographs of the women wading on the shore, exploring the bluffs and reading, all while dressed to the nines in outfits they considered their "island wear." While isolated, they were nonetheless well supplied by passing boats, which also delivered their mail. Like today's visitors to Great Brewster, they relished the views. From their porch, the women "could not only see the Gilded Dome shining like a planet on the horizon, but we could also distinguish the spires of Trinity, the Old South and Brattle St. Churches, while the afternoon sun brought out with equal distinction the Nantasket Shore."

Although both the writing and clothing seemed old-fashioned and quaint, I soon realized that the outing was the equivalent of any modern "Girls' Night Out," a chance for women to kick back and let their hair down. However wealthy these women might have been, they were besieged with the tasks of running households and keeping up social engagements and appearances, just as today's women juggle jobs, caregiving and housework. Like today's campers, the four women felt themselves so close, and yet so far away from it all. In the words of the Scribe:

> It is always an interesting moment…for at the appointed time the light flashes from the Light House, the flag falls from Fort Warren and the sunset gun booms. Music from the excursion boats in the Harbor was wafted to us and we could see the lighted trains of cars crawling to and from Pemberton around Point Allerton and when the friendly lights gleamed all along the horizon from Crescent Beach to Minot's Light, we could not feel that we were far from the Hub of the Universe.

Ironically, Great Brewster may be considered far more isolated today than in 1891, when the women were able to hitch a ride there from a fisherman who lived on the island. Indeed, there were fishing communities on Great Brewster, Middle Brewster and Calf Islands at the time, and Green Island had its own resident hermit for years. For a while in 2002, Great Brewster was served by a boat shuttle from Georges, but for now you have to get there on your own boat or with a tour group.

Luxury on Calf Island

Not all the residents of the Brewsters chose to "rough it" in rustic cabins. At the turn of the twentieth century, railroad and bank director and amateur actor Benjamin P. Cheney bought ten acres on Calf Island, on which he built a mansion for his new bride, the famous actress Julia Arthur. Arthur was, according to a *New York Times* article dated March 30, 1950, "one of the most distinguished actress in the country and abroad." But in 1897, she was also suffering from exhaustion, and the former Ida Lewis was ready to become wife to a millionaire. (The newlywed Cheney did have some unpleasantness from a suit brought by young actress Florence Crosby, who had apparently expected to become Mrs. Cheney, but as Cheney told the *Globe* of November 20, 1899, he "did not leave her penniless, I paid her well. ")

The married couple didn't have to deal with pesky paparazzi as Cheney, who had had a home on Middle Brewster, bought all of Calf Island circa 1900 and built a summer home there as well for him and his betrothed. An August 5, 1903 article in the *New Yorker*, entitled "They Live like Monarchs," described the two-story colonial, dubbed "the Moorings," with its twenty rooms, including a billiard room, study, guest rooms and well-appointed kitchen, complete with silver and linen closets. Rainwater collected on the roof was stored in cisterns for the home's use, and the main living area was flooded with light from lofty windows. Julia Arthur, the article reports, was perfectly content with her home. "If the day be fair, she greets the visitor to 'The Moorings' in a rich gown of immaculate white linen, beautified with Mexican drawn work about the skirt." Mr. Cheney, for his part, "is absolute monarch of all he surveys." The island also featured a garden, a miniature pond, a broad lawn and two Jersey cows.

The Cheneys enjoyed what Julia Arthur called their life of "splendid isolation" for twelve summers. Arthur eventually returned to the stage in 1914 and continued to perform until 1925. Cheney's fortunes had taken a turn for the worse, however, as he had become the target of various lawsuits; in 1917 he was judged to be bankrupt. He died in 1942 at age seventy-six, apparently from thirst; his body was found beside a lonely desert road in Arizona. Arthur died at age eighty-one in 1950. She asked that there be no funeral service, but that her ashes be scattered at sea.

Like so many buildings on the islands, the Cheney mansion slowly crumbled, the victim of time and vandals. Today only a fireplace and chimney mark the Moorings, once, according to the *New Yorker*, "the most sumptuous home about the Hub."

CLIFFS ON THE OUTER BREWSTER, AT LOW TIDE.

An image of the cliffs of Outer Brewster from the 1882 *King's Handbook of Boston Harbor* by M.F. Sweetser, reprinted by the Friends of the Boston Harbor Island. *Courtesy of the Friends of the Boston Harbor Island.*

The Battle of Outer Brewster

In 1936, Edward Rowe Snow declared, "Outer Brewster is, perhaps, the prettiest of all the islands of Boston Harbor. A day spent at this site of chasms and caves will never be forgotten by the visitor."

Seventy years later, the same seventeen-acre island was characterized as a "craggy forlorn outcropping" (*Quincy Patriot Ledger*, October 8, 2005); a "lonely and rarely visited outcrop in the outer harbor" (*Patriot Ledger*, October 28, 2005); and "the backyard of some harbor seals" (*Boston Herald*, July 1, 2006).

What happened to this "prettiest island"? In September 2005, a Virginia energy conglomerate surprised the city of Boston by unveiling a proposal to build a $500 million liquefied natural gas (LNG) terminal on Outer Brewster Island. AES Inc. proposed to build gas tanks in shafts quarried eighty feet into the rock on the north side of the island. Company officials argued that the new terminal, located eight miles offshore, was less of a security risk in the wake of the September 11, 2001 attacks than a facility located near a large population. Moreover, AES declared, it was not out to desecrate a national park; the island had been used previously by the military and was,

During the summer months, ferries to Georges and Spectacle Islands introduce large numbers of visitors to the pleasures of the harbor.

as an AES spokesman put it, "far from a virgin site," according to the *Boston Globe* of September 17, 2005.

Indeed, Outer Brewster had been quite a tramp in her day; during World War II, the army built a gun battery there. The island also houses an abandoned desalination plant, once considered a marvel of military engineering. LNG plan proponents also pointed out that the national park already had equally wayward islands. Consider, they said, the sewage plant on Deer, the fire training and shooting practice sites on Moon and the homeless shelter on Long Island. An LNG terminal on Outer Brewster would fit right in, they declared.

Of course, Outer Brewster was only a mile from Little Brewster and its iconic Boston Light, but AES officials said it "might" not be necessary to establish an "exclusion zone" around the terminal like that required by the U.S. Coast Guard around LNG tankers heading into Boston. Besides, the country needed energy and AES would pay the state $10 million to lease the site. Think of how many park benches that would buy. The plan was for AES to move as much as $3.3 billion worth of natural gas a year through the Outer Brewster terminal into a new undersea pipeline to an existing underwater gas pipeline network.

Because the land of Outer Brewster was still state-owned, the project needed a two-thirds vote by the state legislature before AES could pursue approval from federal officials. Thus, a bill was introduced by State Representative Brian Dempsey calling for the legislature to create a ninety-nine-year lease for the island's use as a liquefied natural gas terminal; the bill's wording disqualified any company except AES from bidding.

Opponents of the project prepared for a battle. "Would the U.S. Park Service or the governor give serious consideration to a plan for the Statue of Liberty to be used as an oil terminal, or Yosemite to store nuclear waste?" fumed an official statement from the Hull Lifesaving Museum. "This wilderness is not an empty wasteland, but a well-protected refuge teeming with flora and wildlife." Park officials said the project would set a dangerous precedent. However, a sweaty and overheated writer griped in an opinion piece in the *Boston Herald* on August 3, 2006, that energy needs were being sacrificed for an island "whose main function now is to serve as an outhouse for gulls."

Outer Brewster does indeed shelter migrating and resident birds, including cormorants, elders, night herons, ibis and oystercatchers, and it is home to a colony of seals as well. At present, such mammals and birds lack personal attorneys to argue their case for life and liberty in a court of law. But they do have the harbor advocates, who proclaimed, "The Harbor Islands are not for sale."

The difficulty of locating a LNG facility in a national park proved too much for AES. In April 2007, the company announced it had withdrawn the proposal. Advocates breathed a sigh of relief. The LNG flap, however, raises larger questions about the proper use and development of the Boston Harbor Islands that future generations will have to answer. A LNG facility may be inappropriate, but what about placing a large windmill (like those in use in Hingham and Hull) on Peddocks or Spectacle to produce alternative energy? As Tom Powers, president of the Boston Harbor Islands Alliance, told me, "We can't say no to everything."

CHAPTER **13**

the strange mercy of rainsford island

In the 1840s, passengers traveling in Boston Harbor would have seen a dramatic sight on a small island north of the Nantasket Roads channel. Perched on a rocky shore was a huge, multistoried stone mansion, ornamented with pillars like a Greek temple. The graceful structure was not, however, the home of a wealthy island dweller. It was a hospital built for unfortunate souls forced into quarantine on a place once called "Hospital Island." Built in 1832, the hospital was criticized for being too expensive and an architectural overkill for a remote island facility. But architect Jotham Rogers apparently believed that the offshore sick deserved the same grandeur afforded to patients treated on the mainland of the "Athens of America."

I first learned about the "Greek Temple" from Elizabeth Carella, a photographic historian who has spent seven years researching this Hospital Island. It bears repeating: The islands speak to visitors in different ways. Edward Rowe Snow had an abiding love of Georges, Sally Snowman felt an instant connection with Little Brewster and Carol Fithian immediately knew she had to rescue the lost boys of Thompson Island. Rainsford Island has its fans and advocates, but chief among them is Carella.

One late afternoon, Carella and I sat down in her apartment overlooking the harbor. As the sun set over Deer Island, we talked about Rainsford's history as a quarantine station, a place where many immigrants to Boston died a painful death from infectious diseases, a few with succor from selfless professionals who believed that the island was, in the words of a poem about the island Carella likes to quote, "mercy's dwelling place." Talking to Carella, who has done a detective's job in pulling out information about Rainsford, I was struck again with a paradox of the island. Rainsford was, in many ways, a dreadful place, a remote location used to isolate

An illustration of a physician boarding a ship to check for infectious diseases from the *King's Handbook of Boston Harbor* by M.F. Sweetser, an 1882 guide to Boston Harbor. *Courtesy of the Friends of the Boston Harbor Island.*

and treat those with yellow fever, smallpox and other diseases. And yet, as Carella has found, many Bostonians sought to ease the suffering of those quarantined with top-notch medical care and professional facilities. They did not always succeed.

Viewed offshore, the 11.4 upland acres of Rainsford present a vision of green. A set of rocky outcroppings just offshore is still called Quarantine Rocks. Edwin Rowe Snow, that energetic teller of tales, said that in the 1820s a "most unusual stone grave" was discovered there, containing a skeleton with an iron sword hilt, "possibly suggesting the burial place of that ancient Norseman Thorwald." Whether or not an ancient Norseman ever visited the island, it's true that Rainsford was settled by Europeans in the seventeenth century. The island was named after an elder of Boston's Old South Church, Edward Rainsford—also spelled Raynsford—who was granted the land for farming in 1636.

From about 1736 to 1847, Rainsford Island was used as a "quarantine station"; in 1737, the official quarantine hospital was moved to Rainsford from Spectacle Island, which was deemed too close to the city. When ships entered Boston Harbor, they would be halted by officials crying out, "Are ye all well on board?" a shout often accompanied by a warning shot if the approaching vessel didn't respond. Ship passengers who had been exposed to disease were forced to come ashore and stay on Rainsford until they recovered, died or otherwise showed no sign of illness.

To decrease the chance of contagion, people would be "treated" with the smoke of burning sulfur, or "smoked with brimstone." Lime and vinegar were applied to ships and their cargo, and hatches, now minus cargo, would be opened to the fresh salt air. In the 1770s, early smallpox inoculations were given on the island by Dr. John Jeffries, the island's quarantine physician, who tested the process on his own seventeen-month-old son At one point, Rainsford had five hospitals, including that dramatic Greek Revival mansion built in 1832 and known throughout the harbor as the "Greek Temple." Famed marine artist Robert Salmon did a dramatic painting of the structure about 1840; it is among the collections of Boston's Museum of Fine Arts. (See color photo number 5.)

The quarantine station was moved to Deer Island in 1847, but public institutions on Rainsford lived on, with the former hospital buildings turned into almshouses and reformatories. The island also held barracks built for disabled veterans of the Civil War. Rainsford even had its own inn, the Old Mansion House, as well as a library. One of the island's caretakers planted a large number of fruit trees, including apple and pear, which bear fruit to this day. Other plantings included a lilac hedge said to be the longest in the Boston area. A piggery provided pork to those on the island and around the harbor. Another landmark on Rainsford was the home of "Portuguese Joe," a house built on stilts on Quarantine Rocks. Joe was a lobsterman who sold his wares on the harbor and was well known around the harbor.

By the 1920s, all the island's institutions had been abandoned, and Portuguese Joe's house was destroyed by fire in the 1930s. Left behind was "historical graffiti" carved into rocks by residents of the island. The island's physician, Dr. J.V.C. Smith, left his name on the island in 1826. Snow records an epitaph that was once cut into a rock on the southwestern side: "Nearby these gray rocks/Enclos'd in a box/Lies Hatter Cox/Who died of small pox." The words themselves, Snow said, were gone, but he provides a photo to show that poor Hatter Cox actually suffered the indignity of a flip rhyme marking her demise.

Nothing remains today of the Greek Temple but its foundations. The hospital burned to the ground in 1918 and was not rebuilt. By 1935, the last remaining building on the island was gutted by fire. Almost nothing but foundations is left, but visitors can still see remains of paths and even of the piggery.

My conversation with Carella turned, as it often does with many island advocates, to what should be done with Rainsford. The island, which is owned by the City of Boston, is technically closed to the public, although private boats do land there. Walking tours are offered from time to time, and Boston's Environment Department has organized cleanups of its shore. Carella worries that additional unsupervised access may mean additional damage to the island, including the threat of fire and litter from careless campers and the painting of the kind of graffiti that is definitely not historical. Still, she wants more people to know about Rainsford's colorful history and the days when suffering immigrants were treated with compassion in a stately building on a remote island. Creating carefully managed public access to Rainsford Island is another challenge facing the national park.

CHAPTER 14

the other long island

It began to reveal itself to them as more than a triangle tip, the lower sections gradually filling in until the sea stretched out flat again on the other side of it and they could see colors filling in as if by brush stroke—a muted green where the vegetation grew unchecked, a tan stripe of shoreline, the dull ochre of cliff face on the northern edge. And at the top, as they churned closer, they began to make out the flat rectangular edges of the buildings themselves.

–Shutter Island, *Dennis Lehane*

Boston Harbor Islands volunteers and national park staff get asked a lot of questions: When's the next boat? How can I get to Boston Light? Where's the bathroom? Given the popularity of local bestselling author Dennis Lehane (*Mystic River*) and the planned Martin Scorsese movie based on Lehane's 2003 thriller *Shutter Island*, I can imagine the volunteers and staff soon rolling their eyes at this one: Where's Shutter Island?

Shutter Island and its Ashecliffe Hospital for the Criminally Insane exist only in the imagination of the Boston-based writer. But Lehane's fictional Shutter Island bears more than a passing resemblance to both Great Brewster Island and another island with a long history of military fortification, lighthouse construction, hospitals and, yes, mental health facilities: Long Island.

Long Island, while part of the national park, is not open to the general public. It currently houses numerous social service programs, including a homeless shelter, treatment programs for substance abuse, a halfway house for former convicts and a locked facility for troubled youth. Every night, homeless individuals in Boston file onto a "Long Island" bus and take a ride over a long bridge and through Moon Island to the facilities on Long Island. Long Island's closed status does not sit well with the island's nearest

The lighthouse
on Long Island,
built in 1901.

neighbors in the city of Quincy, and squabbles between Boston and Quincy
break out with frequency over questions of access and responsibility. Plans
to open a very limited portion of the island sometimes get floated. But for
now, access is limited to clients and professional staff—with one exception.

For many Boston inner city kids, a visit to Long Island may be their first
taste of life on a Boston Harbor Island. In the spring of 2007, with a speed
that astonished most of Boston and confounded many harbor advocates,
a day camp for inner city kids was established on a field on the north side
of Long Island. In about one hundred days, using privately raised funds,
a 14,100-square-foot building, a beach house and pavilions, as well as
basketball courts and playing fields were built. The new Camp Harbor
View does indeed have a spectacular view of the Boston skyline, and several
hundred kids ages eleven to fourteen spent time there in summer 2007.

They had to be transported in minibuses, however, due to concerns over the weight limit on the aging bridge that connects Moon Island to Long Island. The cost of running the camp is to be borne by ongoing corporate donations and private funds.

The day camp seems very much in line with the history of the Harbor Islands as refuges for children in need. In the early twentieth century, poor children were taken by boat out to Bumpkin—many of them so poor they had to be given bathing suits—in the belief that a picnic lunch, outdoor activities and fresh sea air would ward off the miasmas of diseases in inner cities. Today, we hope that the fresh air, bright sunshine and the guidance of adults will protect children from the modern scourge of inner cities—gangs, drugs and street warfare.

Long Island is not only long and narrow—measuring about three-fourths of a mile long and a quarter mile wide—it is the largest of the Harbor Islands, at 225 acres and a high point of 95 feet above sea level. As is true of the other islands, its three drumlins were likely frequented by Native Americans. In the colonial period, the land was used for farming, and the usual squabbles over rightful ownership ensued. In the *King's Handbook of Boston Harbor*, author Sweetser lamented that Long Island was "apportioned to thirty-seven different persons who laid low its beautiful forests and stripped its cliffs bare and desolate." In the nineteenth century, a resort hotel was built on the island and, Sweetser writes, "Occasionally a large assemblage of bruisers and plug-uglies visited Long Island, with the intent to have a comfortable prize-fight; but the police-boat, with a detachment of stalwart officers, as often made a dash on the desecrated island, and prevented the consummation of the affair."

One sunny winter day, I received special permission to visit Long Island. I drove over the causeway linking the mainland to Moon Island, now used as a firefighter training area (where fires are often simulated) and a police firing range. I passed weed-choked concrete vats, the old sewage plant. Before the building of treatment facilities at Deer Island, sewage from the city was processed here, "processed" being a loose term. Huge sewage-holding vats were flushed into the harbor at high tide, expecting the sea to take care of the effluent. Former Boston Fire Chief Leo Stapleton remembers the smell in midsummer at the fire training site as "mind-boggling." Only large slabs of concrete mark the area now, and the air is fresh.

From there, I drove across the two-lane steel bridge, called the Long Island Viaduct, to Long Island, passing a Civil War monument (during that war the island held Camp Wightman, a conscript camp for draftees) and a field now used to grow organic vegetables, which are then served in meals to the homeless and other island clients.

An image of a battery of Fort Strong on Long Island from the 1882 *King's Handbook of Boston Harbor* by M.F. Sweetser. *Courtesy of the Friends of the Boston Harbor Island.*

Just past a rusted, checkered water tower, I reached the main campus, where most of the buildings housing the programs are clustered. Within their brick walls are at least a dozen different programs, including mental health and substance abuse services, detox programs and programs for adolescents. Long Island even has its own Boston Fire Department station, which houses Engine Company 54. Some of the buildings not in use are decaying and crumbling. The once-splendid Curley Building (named after the Boston mayor) is shuttered, but the balcony on its northern side has a magnificent view of the harbor. Another closed building, the former nurses' building, looks like something Dennis Lehane could have invented. Its elegant facade is crumbling, its windows are missing and its walls are latticed with vines, like lines on a wrinkled, leering face. Nearby, battered by wind and sea, is a structure once used as a safe house for informants by Boston police and the FBI. The island's supervisor couldn't tell me which notorious cons had been stashed there. (Well, he could, I suppose. But then he'd have to kill me.)

Some of the buildings on the campus are what's left of the Long Island Chronic Disease Hospital, built about 1882 when the City of Boston took over an old resort hotel on the island and started using it as an almshouse. The city facility was expanded to be used as housing for the homeless as well as a home and hospital for unwed mothers—again keeping with the island's role as a place for things better not spoken of in a less enlightened time. Named with the kind of nineteenth-century directness that would be out of place in the twenty-first century, the Boston Lunatic Hospital also operated here, its unabashed title not unlike Lehane's fictional Ashecliffe Hospital for the Criminally Insane. Yet Long was considered a place of hope and recovery, with a sturdy, quaint chapel for people of all faiths. Photographs, circa 1890, of one of the island's hospitals show clean, spare and sunlight-drenched wards, staffed by crisply dressed nurses.

In the early 1800s, a Portuguese fishing community sprang up along the shore of Long Island. But they were forced to leave as the city continued to increase its facilities for institutional care on the island. So in the 1880s, the fishermen floated many of their homes to Peddocks Island, where they again created a community.

Just northeast from the main campus is Camp Harbor View, set against a dazzling backdrop of sea and sky amid playing fields. Those fields, built on the parade grounds of the former Fort Strong, are guarded by several fake coyotes that seem to be keeping the (very real) and constantly pooping Canada geese at bay. From the fields, you can catch a glimpse of the top of the fifty-two-foot Long Island Head lighthouse, also called the Inner Harbor Light. This light station, first established in 1819, was moved about the island to accommodate military fortifications; the whitewashed structure with the black top that boat passengers can see from the water was built in 1901. Long Island Head received a major renovation in 1998, and it now flashes every 2.5 seconds under automated solar power. A bunker set in the hill below Long Island Head has been fitted with some incongruous bright pink shutters.

The remains of Fort Strong today on Long Island.

Much of the northeastern tip of Long Island is taken up by the remains of Fort Strong, a maze of twisting pillars and posts, overrun with prickly vines and bittersweet with rusted ladders leading to nowhere. The island was used as a training camp for Civil War draftees, and in 1867 Fort Strong was moved here from Noddles Island and built up during the Endicott period. Fort Strong played a role in overseeing the placement of mines in the harbor, strategically positioned to ward off enemy ships but avoid decimating local fishermen. After World War II, the fort was decommissioned. However, in the 1950s, the island was brought into the Cold War with the placement of a Nike missile base here. Also about 1950, the bridge linking Moon and Long Islands to the mainland was built, ending Long Island's status as an isolated island. When the Nike missiles were removed, the empty silos were used to store books from the Boston Public Library.

Today Fort Strong's batteries, former gun emplacements, bunkers and storage areas are weatherworn and cracked. Trees, once gone from the island, have returned with a vengeance and are making up for lost time by seeking to fill every inch of space around the fort. Watchtowers, now marked with graffiti and crumbling under the slow pressure of roots and plants, gaze over a harbor that has become a recreational zone, not a potential battlefield.

And what would a Boston Harbor Island be without its own ghost story? Courtesy of Edward Snow, there's the tale of the Lady in Scarlet. In 1776, during hostilities between Patriot troops and a British fleet, William Burton and his wife Mary Burton were caught in the bombardment while visiting a British craft. Mortally wounded by a cannonball, Mary begged her husband to bury her on dry land. William promised and buried his wife on Long Island, sewn into a red blanket. Since then fishermen and soldiers have seen the form of a woman, wearing a scarlet cloak, moaning and wailing. Snow, naturally, offers no independent verification of the event.

Over the years, as the needs of the city have shifted, various ideas have been put forward as to how best to use Long Island. In the mid-1990s, construction mogul and megalomaniac Donald Trump decided it would be a great idea to build a casino on Long Island. While it's unclear whether the city ever took the proposal that seriously, representatives of "the Donald" announced they would craft a plan to put a casino, private house and marina on the island. In the end, the proposal never got off the ground. The communities of Quincy and Boston continue to wrangle over access to Long Island (in July of 1992, hundreds defiantly flocked to its shore to get a glimpse of the tall ships then visiting Boston Harbor), and the bridges linking Moon and Long Islands to the mainland are in need of repair.

The mythical Shutter Island may have its mysteries, but they pale in comparison with the real story of Boston's Long Island.

CHAPTER 15

the once and former islands

You have read my mantra: You don't need your own boat to enjoy the Boston Harbor Islands. Here's another one: You don't even need to get *on* a boat to enjoy the Boston Harbor Islands. A number of the "islands" in the national park are *former* islands, places now connected by land to the mainland and accessible to the public by automobile and, for the hearty, bicycle. While not as remote as the "real" islands, these former islands have historical importance and natural beauty in abundance. We will start north and work our way south.

The Dinosaur Eggs of Deer Island

Looking like the headquarters of super villain Dr. Evil, the island's bulbous towers rise up, one after the other, 170 feet into the air. I pump my bike, urging my old muscles to get with it as I head by these mammoth "digesters," part of the Deer Island sewage treatment plant that has, in no small measure, saved Boston Harbor.

I'm here at the urging of many who have told me that one of the best ways to experience Boston Harbor is by a bike ride or walk around Deer Island. "You want me to ride around a sewage plant?" I asked incredulously. Just do it, I am told. So here I am, navigating the cement paths that circle and crisscross the "island," now connected to the mainland. My heart banging in my chest, I head for the bend at the southeast point of the island. As I pump the pedals, my eyes drift past the railing of the path to the unbroken line of ocean horizon to the east. Looking southwest, I see the skyline of the city of Boston, and Long and Spectacle Islands. I can also take side trails that cut up hills to historical markers and lookouts. Close up,

The mammoth "digesters" that help process the sewage at the Deer Island treatment plant may look ominous, but they have helped to clean up a harbor that was once a national disgrace.

the giant digesters—which are visible from all over the Harbor Islands and are often dubbed the "dinosaur eggs" by rangers—have a faintly ominous appearance. Yet they represent the rebirth of the harbor, as they do their job, day in and day out, of controlling the vast amount of sewage and waste produced by the city's population.

On this afternoon, I'm not alone; lots of people in the nearby town of Winthrop and beyond have realized that Deer Island is a great place for a walk, run or jog. They tell me that, yes, at times, there can be an odor, very strong at times. But if you turn your back to the plant and keep your eyes toward the water, the experience of Deer Island is not that much different than the description written in the 1880s by M.F. Sweetser in his *King's Handbook of Boston Harbor*: "The drive around the island is everywhere beautiful, with the deep blue of the sea stretching out beyond, the distant isles dotted over the bay, and the white sails of vessels appearing on the horizon, returning home from distant ports." Still there is a shadow over Deer Island that has nothing to do with sewage. Even in the long history of the Boston Harbor Islands as places of misery or last resort, Deer Island has housed more than its share of despair.

Millie McGowan, a member of the Nipmuc nation, Natick Band, is a descendant of the "praying Indians" who were relocated to Deer Island during King Philip's War. *Courtesy of Boston Harbor Islands Alliance.*

It was dubbed Deer Island in colonial times, when deer from the mainland would swim out to its shores. In those days, the island was separated only by a narrow channel of water, called Shirley's Gut, from what is now the town of Winthrop.

The island figures in a particularly cruel moment in the history of America's native people. When in 1675 a native sachem, or chief, decided to fight back against the ever-increasing number of European settlers in the area, one of the bloodiest conflicts in early American history ensued. That conflict was called King Philip's War, after another name for Metacomet, a leader of the Wampanoag who formed alliances with other native groups to fight the intruders. By this time, however, a number of natives had converted to Christianity under the guidance of Roxbury minister John Eliot, and many were living in a settlement in Natick, a town some miles west of Boston. These so-called "praying Indians" were not part of Metacomet's movement, but were still deemed a potential threat by frightened white settlers. An estimated five hundred to one thousand mostly women and children were forcibly moved to Deer Island and held captive without adequate food, clothing or shelter. Details of the exact death toll are sketchy, but at least half of the uprooted natives died over the winter. King Philip's War ended with the death of Metacomet in 1676, and gradually the native people on Deer were allowed to leave; some may have been sold into slavery, while others were able to return to other native communities.

The legacy of this seventeenth-century internment camp became an issue in the creation of the Boston Harbor Island National Park Area. Native Americans consider Deer Island a sacred place because it was the site of their ancestors' suffering. When the national park was created, a decision was made to call it a "park area" rather than a "recreation area," in consideration of the events of 1675. Today, Native Americans hold ceremonies on the island to remember its victims. In an educational DVD, *Living in Two Worlds: Native American Voices on the Boston Harbor Islands*, produced in 2006 by National Park Service staff, the Boston Harbor Islands Alliance and World Turtle Productions, Millie McGowan, a member of the Nipmuc nation, Natick Band, explains her feelings about Deer Island: "This island is a very, very important place for me. Sometimes when I walk here, I can feel the spirits, and I believe they walk with me. I think it's important that we all acknowledge what has happened here, because for many, many years no one wanted to speak about what happened here."

Other miseries continued into the next few centuries. In 1847, a quarantine hospital was established on Deer Island that treated nearly five thousand people, including immigrants fleeing the Irish potato famine as well as folks on the mainland who developed smallpox or other infectious diseases. Deer Island is also considered historically significant in the long history of the Irish immigration to Boston. The island once had two cemeteries, one for prisoners and hospital patients and the other for military personnel, including Confederate soldiers imprisoned in Fort Warren.

In the late 1850s, a house of reformation was established, its beds and cells filled with what Sweetser called the "army of the criminal class." This house of reformation eventually became a "house of correction," or a prison, one of the largest in the state, which held many of the era's notorious criminals, including members of the gang that robbed the Brink's armored car company in 1950. The Deer Island House of Correction closed in 1991. When Shirley Gut, the stretch of water that once separated Deer Island from the mainland, was closed up by New England's famous Hurricane of 1938, Deer Island became an island in name only.

In the mid-1980s, Boston Harbor was the very symbol of pollution. In the 1988 presidential campaign, George Bush Sr. successfully torpedoed Michael Dukakis's environmental credentials with a boat ride through Boston Harbor that highlighted its polluted state. (Dukakis's joy ride in a tank didn't help much either.) Ironically, by then forces were in place to clean up the

Annawon Weedon, a member of the Mashpee Wampanoag nation, helps a visitor learn a native craft on Spectacle Island.

harbor. In 1985, U.S. District Court Judge Paul Garrity—known afterward as the "sludge judge"—ordered the cleanup of Boston Harbor after ruling that the wastewater being dumped into it violated the 1972 Federal Clean Water Act. The newly formed Massachusetts Water Resources Authority began work on what was to become a state-of-the-art treatment plant on Deer Island, replacing another treatment facility that had been built early in the century. Four billion dollars later, the harbor is no longer a national embarrassment. Some might even say the water is clean.

Today, the treatment plant takes up about two-thirds of the island's 185 upland acreage. About 60 acres are open for walking, bike riding, picnicking and fishing. Signs explain the process of sewage treatment and commemorate the Native American and Irish experiences here. A memorial for the Native American detainees is planned. For a time, ferries headed to Georges Island made stops at Deer Island to encourage visitation; security concerns after 2001 put a stop to that. However, you can reach Deer Island by driving through the town of Winthrop and parking at the gate leading

Looking out from a massive doorway of Fort Independence on Castle Island in South Boston.

into the plant. The pathways are well marked. Keep your eyes on the horizon and you might think you are way out in the harbor on a true island, even if the air has a "funny" smell once in a while.

Tours of the Deer Island facilities are available during warm months; make an appointment via www.mwra.com or call 617.660.7607.

Castle Island

After work (or when I could sneak away at noon), I would maneuver my way through the streets of South Boston (with its quaint custom of double parking) to Castle Island for a run. I would park on L Street and run to Day Boulevard, urging my muscles along the waterside sidewalk. I would take a right onto the causeway that juts into the harbor and over to Castle Island and Fort Independence, a nineteenth-century fortification. Ignoring the teenagers and seventy-somethings racing past me, I would gulp in the bracing air and somehow draw energy from the waves around me as I panted my way around the broad sidewalk that circles the island.

Due to the many landfill projects that have expanded the borders of South Boston considerably, Castle Island is the least island-like of the once and former islands in the harbor. Indeed, I had been running there for years before I learned that its name was not just a quirky misnomer. Castle Island is not part of the Boston Harbor Islands National Park, but I include it here because its history is so linked with the harbor. Except on extremely harsh winter days, the path around the island (now part of Boston's Harbor Walk trail) is filled with people: women pushing baby carriages and talking animatedly, older gentlemen in sweats and Red Sox hats, kamikaze bike riders, kids pulling—or being pulled by—big dogs. When you get to the eastern edge of the park, the views of Spectacle Island, of planes taking off and landing at Logan Airport, of the commuter boats making their daily journeys and even of Boston Light winking from the horizon may make you feel you have left Boston behind. Aiding in that impression is a tall obelisk that overlooks the harbor, a monument to Donald McKay, a famous Boston shipbuilder. The monument is decorated with a bas-relief of the *Great Republic*, the largest ship in the world when launched on October 4, 1853, at a length of 325 feet.

Fort Independence itself, with its granite walls topped by earthwork, rises imposingly on a slight hill. Various forts were built on this location starting in 1634, for the sea defense of Boston. A four-bastioned fort finished in 1703 was known as Castle William, after William III of Orange, the British king. That one lasted until 1776, when British troops returned cannon fire at the American revolutionaries occupying nearby Dorchester Heights. The British cannons, however, could not reach the Patriots, and a British cannon exploded at the fort, the only hostile action its ramparts ever saw.

By March of that same year, the British had had it with the pesky American insurgents and decided it was time to declare "victory" and get out. This move on their part is still celebrated in Boston on March 17, under the antiseptic name of Evacuation Day. Evacuation Day falls—coincidentally—on St. Patrick's Day. (Creating Evacuation Day was a shrewd move by Irish politicians in 1901, making St. Patrick's Day an official holiday.) On the first Evacuation Day, the British destroyed Castle Island's fortifications and, for good measure, the Boston Light lighthouse, on their way out of town. The fort was quickly repaired, and during the Revolutionary War, American companies were trained there. The current structure, the island's seventh fort, was built between 1801 and 1803. The five-sided, five-bastion brick fort doubled the former's height and expanded its perimeter; the brick was later replaced with granite from Maine quarries.

Like Fort Warren on Georges Island, Fort Independence has its legends. On the dawn of Christmas Day in 1817, sword in hand, Army Second Lieutenant Robert F. Massie stepped onto a granite rampart overlooking the harbor to fight a duel with Lieutenant Gustavus Drane, who had accused Massie of cheating at cards the night before. The pair fought, and

Drane dispatched Massie with a sword thrust into his chest. Drane was court-martialed for the duel, but no other officers would testify against him. Massie was buried at the site of the duel, and his friends put up a handsome marble gravestone to mark the spot. However, as the rumor goes, Massie's friends decided to exact revenge by catching Drane while he was drunk and walling him up alive in the fort. Ten years later, in 1927, poet and writer Edgar Allen Poe served five months at Fort Warren, under the name of Edgar Perry. (He was then attempting to elude various creditors.) Intrigued by the tale, Poe turned the duel and its supposed aftermath into his classic short story "The Cask of Amontillado," in which a man lures his enemy into a cellar with the promise of fine liquor and walls him up alive behind bricks.

Well and good, but actually Drane was promoted after the duel, married, died of natural causes and was buried outside Philadelphia. So if there is any veracity to the story of this unnatural burial, it did not involve him. There are, however, repeated references to this story. In 1905, workers repairing the masonry at Fort Independence broke through a wall and found a skeleton wearing the remains of a uniform from the early 1800s. Edward Rowe Snow may be the source of this tale; he reported that when "talking with an elderly man at the island some years ago," Snow learned that workmen opening up a wall that had been closed for

Scenes from Nut Island from the 1882 *King's Handbook of Boston Harbor* by M.F. Sweetser. *Courtesy of the Friends of the Boston Harbor Island.*

many years found "a skeleton dressed in an old military costume." Snow also reports that the stone marking Massie's grave was eventually moved to Fort Devens in Ayer.

Castle Island has inspired even more tall tales, including the sighting of a sea serpent off its shores. With its cannons poking from the top of the parapets, its rusty grates, narrow windows and stained granite, Fort Independence does seem like a place where ghosts would stalk. Or jog.

Castle Island is accessible via Day Boulevard in South Boston.

Nut Island

Like Deer Island, the small Nut Island is the site of a waste treatment facility, but its grounds have been turned into a park that provides great views of the harbor. Sewage is pumped from the Nut Island Headworks through a 4.8-mile tunnel that runs under the harbor to Deer Island for treatment.

Once connected to the mainland only at low tide, Nut Island was used for cattle grazing by colonists. It was supposedly named for a lone nut tree that grew on its four acres, but it was also called Hoff's Thumb and Hough's Tomb. A monument created with pieces of artillery shells testifies to the island's use as a testing ground for heavy ordnance in the 1800s. Shells were fired across the water at bluffs on Peddocks Island, not always finding their mark, according to *King's Handbook of Boston Harbor*. One four-hundred-pound shot reportedly landed in a hillside cemetery in Hull, to the consternation of Hull citizens.

Today the guns are silent. A fishing pier, plus numerous benches set among replanted trees, make Nut Island a pleasant spot for a picnic.

Nut Island is now connected by land to Houghs Neck in Quincy and can be accessed by car by following Sea Street from Route 3A.

Webb Memorial State Park

If there are lost islands in the Boston Harbor Islands National Park, there are also rescued islands. One is Spectacle, and another is the peninsula of Webb Memorial State Park, once the location of weapons of mass destruction and now a favorite spot for walkers, joggers and kite flyers. Its thirty-six acres have trails and numerous memorials, including one with the gentle reminder to "Love One Another" etched into its granite.

The park comprises two drumlins that were used by Native Americans for gathering shellfish, finfish and wild fruit. Europeans used the area for

A view of the Boston Harbor Islands taken from Worlds End.

farming until 1872, when the Bradley Fertilizer Company took over the area with a large complex of buildings. In the late 1950s, the area became a Nike missile base. The missiles were controlled and tracked from a location at Fort Duvall on Little Hog Island (since turned into the condo-complex development of Spinnaker Island). Fortunately, much like the guns on the many forts in Boston Harbor, the Nike missiles were never used in an attack. In 1974, the Nike site was dismantled and the land was acquired by the Commonwealth of Massachusetts. After a major cleanup, the area became Webb Memorial State Park and later part of the national park. In the summer, it is awash with yellow yarrow and many determined joggers bent on shedding those persistent pounds. Cleanup work of the contamination caused by the former fertilizer plant continues.

Webb Memorial State Park is accessible by automobile from River Street off Route 3A in Weymouth.

Worlds End

Has there ever been a more evocative name for a park than "Worlds End"? On a blustery winter day, when the park has few visitors and the wind sounds like a freight train as it thrashes the trees, I take a walk through its hills and meadows, feeling like I am heading to the part of the map marked "Here Be Dragons." My hood pulled close around my head, I climb a path leading to the top of one of the four drumlins in the park. I hear a redtail hawk screech, a haunting sound that is weirdly familiar. It is used as a stand-in for an eagle's call on TV's *The Colbert Report*. With apologies to Stephen Colbert's faux eagle, nothing compares to a real cry from a real hawk. I see one, then two more hawks circling overhead, in their endless hunt for food.

I follow one of several paths that begin at the small guardhouse at Martin's Cove, the park's entrance. The two southern drumlins of the park are a peninsula connected to the South Shore town of Hingham, with Hingham Harbor on one side and Porter's Cove on the other. At one time the area that is now Damde Meadows was a salt marsh that cut off the island from the mainland twice a day. It was dammed to create a hay meadow; currently the area is being slowly returned to a salt marsh. The twin northern drumlins, connected now to the southern portion by a small land bar, were once their own island. This is the section properly called Worlds End, a name that has come to refer to the entire 248-acre park. The narrow land bar was built by early settlers to gain access to the island for farming. Along the shore, a flock of black and white bufflehead ducks float, their bills tucked into their backs, snoozing as they drift. A flicker of blue catches my eye as a bluebird flits by. The leafless trees reveal abandoned nests, one intricately woven and hung between two branches with the delicacy of an artist.

Majestic trees line the pathways or form thick groves. In the late nineteenth century, however, only three trees—elms—were left of the forest that covered the area when Europeans first arrived. All the area on this peninsula had been cleared for farming. Now there's a mixture of forest and meadow, crisscrossed with curious old stone fences. From vantage points thoughtfully provided with benches, I can look out to Bumpkin and Peddocks Islands and to the skyline of Boston beyond them. It's very lucky that I can walk here at all. This land, now thick with trees and home to hawks, was once slated for development, ranging from country estates to the headquarters of the United Nations to a nuclear power plant.

No one seems to know officially where the name "Worlds End" came from. But we do know that from 1855 to 1882, John R. Brewer of Boston, a gentleman farmer, began buying up land between the Weir River and Hingham Harbor and along a road called Martin's Lane. He built a large home and ran a larger farming operation here, growing corn, oats, sugar beets, alfalfa and vegetables, and keeping considerable numbers of sheep, cows and horses. He also bought up nearby Langlee and Sarah Islands. (These islands were later obtained by the town of Hingham and are now part of the national park.) The Brewer family seemed to have a particular fondness for their horses, which were, according to *A History of World's End* by William H.C. Walker and Willard Brewer Walker, given names starting with a different letter of the alphabet for each year they were obtained. One little bay mare was known lovingly as Pet. "Indeed," write the authors of the Worlds End history, "the farm clung stubbornly to horses and as late as the mid 1930s, operated without a single gasoline-powered vehicle."

About 1886, Brewer retained the services of famed landscape architect Frederick Law Olmsted, the man responsible for Boston's "Emerald Necklace" series of parks. Brewer wanted to subdivide the area past Martin's Cove into 163 lots. Accordingly, Olmsted drew up a plan with undulating, tree-lined roads snaking through the areas of Planter's Hill, Rocky Neck and Worlds End proper, and included a spot for a "Brewer Grove." By 1900, the roads were laid out and the trees planted, but the subdivision was never made. Brewer died in 1893, and while the farm continued to operate, his last child died in 1936, and the property was acquired in 1944 by Helen Brewer Walker.

In 1945, a Massachusetts committee proposed that Worlds End (along with other sites) be considered as a location for the fledgling United Nations (eventually located in New York City). In 1965, a New England electric company considered locating a nuclear power plant in Worlds End; the plant was built instead in Plymouth. Eventually, the land was acquired by the Trustees of Reservations, a conservation group, formed in 1891 to protect and preserve Massachusetts land. The group oversees about ninety-four such "reservations," and the Worlds End park is one of its crown jewels.

Today, you can ramble along the roads designed by Olmsted or meander along the shore. The Rocky Neck area has sweeping views of the harbor and a curious ice pond to explore. The park is big enough to get lost in—a remarkable achievement on my part during a recent visit, since I was clutching one of the maps provided at the entrance. A popular spot, Worlds End is often filled with visitors on weekends and holidays. If you happen to catch a winter sunset there, which often ignites the sky with neon orange and crimson, and transforms the water at the land's end with reflective glory, you may start to believe that you are standing at the edge of the world, or at least the part where the map ends.

To reach Worlds End, take Route 3A to Summer Street in Hingham; turn left on Martin's Lane. For information, go to www.thetrustees.org or call 781.740.6665.

CHAPTER 16

the future of the boston harbor islands

The Boston Harbor Islands National Park Area remains a work in progress. The islands are continually changing due to both the forces of nature and human design. Through deliberate purpose and inadvertent neglect, the islands are starting to resemble the wild, green places Europeans saw when they first came to North American shores. "The islands are now more natural than at any other time after the arrival of the colonists," as a park ranger told me. Once again, the islands are places of exploration and relaxation, while their history and biology continue to attract research and scholarship.

But we humans still have a lot of work to do. While there have been notable successes—the opening of Spectacle Island among them—there also have been setbacks for the national park. Historic buildings, particularly on Peddocks, continue to deteriorate. Gallops remains closed due to asbestos concerns. Boat transportation to the islands continues to experience ups and downs, with long lines and circuitous routes that often leave a wake of frazzled visitors. Many who profess their love for the islands often disagree on how to best express that love in the actual management of the park.

Many praise the comprehensive General Master Plan issued in 2003 by the Islands Partnership, which outlines lofty goals for each island. The plan envisions "actors reading excerpts from the soldiers' journals" among the old forts of the islands. It imagines science programs for students who, aboard a laboratory boat, take water measurements; catch, examine and return sea creatures; and analyze data. In campsites throughout the islands, visitors "marvel at the diversity of the campers they meet…a couple from Sweden, a family with three young children from Oregon, a boy scout troop from New Hampshire, and many people from neighborhoods of Boston." A ranger with theatrical skills tells ghost stories to assembled families around a crackling fire: "The program is a hit with the campers, who despite the ghoulish tales, feel secure and safe

Boston Light, Boston Har

A postcard of
Boston Light at
night, circa 1910.
*Courtesy of Kathy
Alpert.*

on the island as they make their way back to their campsites. The night sky is exceptionally clear, and the families from Boston remark on how rare it is to see such darkness."

Immediate plans call for refurbishing a visitors' center on Georges Island and adding a new kayaking program. A "harbor park pavilion visitor contact station" that will tell tourists about what lies just off shore is planned for the new Rose Fitzgerald Kennedy Greenway in downtown Boston.

Many have imagined what the park could be one day. However, "Today is that day," as a DCR official told me. "We all know what needs to be done. Gallops needs to be opened. We need funding, funding, funding." At times, however, the clamor from the various constituencies gets overwhelming. "It's a contest to see who cares the most," the official griped. "Instead of complaining, some might ask, 'What can I do to really help?'"

True, advocates can be a pain in the rear. But transparency and an interested public will only improve the park's prospects. Various park officials have given me a good sense of the demanding nature of their jobs, but I have been chilled by the implicit threat that pops up at times: If something gets too much to handle, we'll just close it down. That's not a happy thought. More islands need to be opened up, not fewer.

You, the reader, can help. If you've never visited the islands, venture out, more than once. (See your "homework assignment" in the next chapter). Tell park officials—politely—of your impressions. Every year, more people are rediscovering the Boston Harbor Islands. Every year, a few more hear the seductive call of one of them, whispering, "This is *your* island." This summer, take a trip into the harbor, do some island hopping and listen to what the islands say to you.

CHAPTER 17

your homework assignment

Ten Things to Do on the
Boston Harbor Islands This Summer

Now that you've come to the end of this book, here is your assignment:

1. View Boston Light from Fort Warren on Georges Island.
2. Meditate on the meaning of life on an overlook on Grape Island.
3. Hike the length of Peddocks *and* manage to catch the last ferry off the island.
4. Visit the children's graveyard on Thompson Island.
5. Watch the land bridge that leads from Bumpkin to Hull rise out of the water during low tide.
6. Climb to the top of the southern drumlin on Spectacle Island. Or the northern drumlin. Or both.
7. Take a boat tour to Little Brewster to see Boston Light up close and personal
8. Ride a bike around Deer Island.
9. Picnic at Worlds End.
10. Watch the sun set behind Boston from Lovells Island.

sources

Books

Baker, William A. *A History of the Boston Marine Society 1742–1967*. Boston: Boston Marine Society, 1968.

Connelly, Patrick J. *Islands of Boston Harbor 1630 to 1932, "Green Isles of Romance."* Dorchester, MA: Chapple Publishing Company, LTD, 1932.

D'Etremont, Jeremy. *The Lighthouses of Massachusetts*. Beverly, MA: Commonwealth Editions, 2007.

Green, James. *Hangman: A Tale of the Boston Harbor Islands*. Bloomington, IN: 1st Books, 2003.

Jennings, Harold B. *A Lighthouse Family*. Orleans, MA: Lower Cape Pub. Co., 1989.

Kales, David. *The Boston Harbor Islands: A History of an Urban Wilderness*. Charleston, SC: The History Press, 2007.

———. *The Phantom Pirate: Tales of the Irish Mafia and the Boston Harbor Islands*. Bloomington, IN: AuthorHouse, 2004.

Kales, Emily, and David Kales. *All About the Boston Harbor Islands*. Fourth and Revised Edition. Cataumet, MA: Hewitts Cove Publishing Co., Inc., 1993.

Lehane, Dennis. *Shutter Island*. New York: HarperCollins, 2003.

Mallory, Ken, ed. *Boston Harbor Islands National Park Area*. Camden, ME: Down East Books, 2003.

Mikal, Alan. *Exploring Boston Harbor in Photographs and Text*. North Quincy, MA: The Christoper Publishing House, 1973.

Morss, Sherman, Jr. *Boston Harbor Islands*. Beverly, MA: Commonwealth Editions, 2005.

Perkins, William D. *Chestnuts, Galls, and Dandelion Wine: Useful Wild Plants of the Boston Harbor Islands*. Halifax, MA: The Plant Press, 1982.

Quinn, William P. *Shipwrecks Around Boston*. Hyannis, MA: Parnassus Imprints, 1996.

Schmidt, Jay. *Fort Warren: New England's Most Historic Civil War Site*. Amherst, NH: UBT Press, 2003.

Shurtleff, Nathaniel Bradstreet. *A Topographical and Historical Description of Boston*. Third Edition. Boston: Published by Order of the Common Council, 1891.

Silvia, Matilda. *Once Upon an Island*. Cohasset, MA: Hot House Press, 1993.

Snowman, Sally R., and James G. Thomson. *Boston Light: A Historical Perspective*. Plymouth, MA: Flagship Press, 1999.

Stapleton, Leo D. *Thirty Years on the Line*. Boston: Quinlan Publishing Company, Inc., 1982.

Stark, James. *Illustrated History of Boston Harbor*. Boston: Photo-Electrotype Co., 1879.

Stephens, Alexander. *Recollections of Alexander H. Stephens: His Diary Kept When a Prisoner at Fort Warren, Boston Harbour, 1865*. Baton Rouge: Louisiana State University Press, 1998.

Sullivan, Robert F. *Shipwrecks and Nautical Lore of Boston Harbor: A Mariner's Chronicle of More Than 100 Shipwrecks, Heroic Rescues and Salvage Accounts, Treasure Tales, Island Legends, and Harbor Anecdotes*. Chester, CT: The Globe Pequot Press, 1990.

Sweetser, M.F. *King's Handbook of Boston Harbor*. Boston: A Friends of the Boston Harbor Islands Inc., Publication, reprinted, 1882.

Walker, William H.C., and Willard Brewer Walker. *A History of World's End*. Second edition. Milton, MA: The Trustees of Reservations, 1973.

Other Sources

Advisory Council Analysis of the Boston Harbor National Park Area Five Year Strategic Plan, March 1, 2006.

Articles in the *Boston Globe, Boston Herald, Quincy Patriot-Ledger* and other Massachusetts newspapers, 1786 to 2008.

Baptista, Robert J. "Albert C. Burrage biography," September 6, 2006, www.colorantshistory.org/AlbertBurrageBio.html.

Boston Harbor Islands General Management Plan, prepared by the Boston Support Office of the Northeast Region National Park Service for the Boston Harbor Islands Partnership, 2002.

"Boston Harbor Islands National Park Area: Natural Resources Overview." *Northeastern Naturalist* 12, Special Issue 3 (2005).

Enos, Robert F. "Peddock's." Paper for Master of Fine Arts in Design, Southeastern Massachusetts University, May 6, 1986.

Harvard College Class of 1883, fourth report, 1890 to 1900, Cambridge, MA, S.N. 1900 [?].

Peddocks Island: Building Conditions Assessment for Fort Andrews and Island Cottages. Prepared by the Massachusetts Department of Conservation and Recreation, September 2007.

Odyssey School at South Boston High Presents: Adventures on the Boston Harbor Islands. Summer 2003 edition.

WGBH Forum Network, archived webcasts of lectures.
———. Military History of the Boston Harbor Islands, May 28, 2003, forum.wgbh.org/wgbh/forum.php?lecture_id=1248.

———. Rainsford Island: Resort to Reformatory, May 14, 2003, forum. wgbh.org/wgbh/forum.php?lecture_id=1252.

Sources

————. Ten Years of Progress: Boston Harbor Islands National Park, June 26, 2006, forum.wgbh.org/wgbh/forum.php?lecture_id=3152.

————. What Lies Beneath: Sunken Treasure in Boston Harbor, Thursday, March 22, 2007, forum.wgbh.org/wgbh/forum.php?search=gontz&x =0&y=0.

Whittier, Helen Augusta, diary. "Ye Log of Ye Square Partie at Ye Great Brewster, Pleasant Month of July 1891." Schlesinger Library, Radcliffe College, Cambridge, MA.

about the author

Stephanie Schorow, a Boston-area writer, is the author of *The Crime of the Century: How the Brink's Robbers Stole Millions and the Hearts of Boston*, *Boston on Fire: A History of Fires and Firefighting in Boston* and *The Cocoanut Grove Fire*. She was the editor and project coordinator for *Boston's Fire Trail: A Walk through the City's Fire and Firefighting History*, published by The History Press. She has worked as a reporter for the *Boston Herald* and the Associated Press; her articles now appear regularly in the *Boston Globe* and other publications.

The author on Lovells Island in 2007. *Photo by Marsha Turin.*

Visit us at
www.historypress.net